HOLDING BREATH

A Memoir of AIDS' Wildfire Days

By Nancy Bevilaqua

"Streets Of Philadelphia" by Bruce Springsteen. Copyright © 1993 Bruce Springsteen (ASCAP). Reprinted by permission. International copyright secured. All rights reserved.

Days of the Dead "solitary soul" quote is from _Hanal Pixan_ Yesterday and Today: The Mayan Ritual of the Dead, 1ˢᵗ ed. (Merida, Yucatan, Mexico: _Editorial Dante_, 2004), David Phillips, trans.

Definition of "disenfranchised guilt" by Kathleen R. Gilbert, Professor and Associate Dean at Indiana University, used by permission.

"The Lover Who Did Not Come" (_A loon/I thought it was…_) (Ojibway), Frances Densmore, trans. (Chippewa Music II. _Bulletin 53_. Washington: Bureau of American Ethnology, 1913)

TABLE OF CONTENTS

PART ONE:
INTRODUCTION/AWAKENED

Last night I dreamed about a kiss that never happened, sixteen years ago. The kiss came at the end of a long tangle of images involving hospital hallways and rooms, patients, some sense of danger, and a need to escape. It came as an inevitability, an opportunity finally taken when, in reality, it's too late. David's mouth was opened in an O; it was battered and decayed as I knew it would be, and I had a fleeting thought about his illness, but I wanted that kiss. There the dream ended, and I woke up with the sweet, aching sense of longing that I get after dreaming about being in love. The feeling was like a thin piece of tissue that I tried to hold onto all day, knowing full well that by evening it would have dissolved from the sheer pressure of my holding it so tightly.

The sun is now setting, and the mourning doves are calling their goodbyes, and the feeling is gone.

That—a dream scrawled into my long-neglected journal one morning while I was still in bed at my family's summer house in Hampton Bays, on Long Island—was what started to wake me up; I'd been sleepwalking for sixteen years. I don't know how long it had been since the last time I'd dreamt about David; I can only guess that being in that house on an early-summer morning in 2006 stirred back up to the reachable places of my dreaming mind the memory of the prematurely hot May day in 1990 on which I'd gone out onto the lawn in front of the house and buried his ashes, alone, with only the squawking of some blue jays and the drone of traffic on Montauk Highway as funeral hymns.

It wasn't that I'd forgotten him. There had been many times in those sixteen years when I'd passed

7

that place in the lawn and silently said hello to him, as if it would be his ashes that would hear me. I'd told my husband and my son about him, and sometimes something that David had said, or a certain look on his face, would flicker in my memory and then fade again.

He hadn't wanted to be forgotten, and I never meant to forget him. But sixteen years had passed, and many things had happened in my life since that May morning. Until I had the dream, I'd been in danger of forgetting completely that I'd been in love with him, and what his death had done to me.

It almost seems strange that I could forget that I'd loved David, but maybe it had been what I'd needed to do. My husband, whom I'd met and married four years after David's passing, suspected it before I remembered myself. "You were in love with him, weren't you?" he'd say, and I'd deny it over and over, believing, somehow, what I told him—that David had been a dying man in no condition for love, a heroin addict with AIDS for whom sex was almost as remote a possibility as survival, and that I was simply there to see him through to the end, in as much comfort as possible, because there was no one else. I may even have admitted out loud my belief at that point (which may have in fact been at least part of the truth at the beginning) that it was through David that I'd lived out my own unimaginative fantasy of being someone's savior, someone's angel, someone's last hope.

As it turned out, the process of finding him again was even more painful than the slow, inevitable ordeal of losing him had been.

The Box

Shortly after I had the dream on Long Island, back at home in New Jersey, I pulled out my journal from my time with David, which I kept in a box with the folded flag that his veteran friends had presented to me at the memorial service I'd managed to cobble together for him, his Patient I.D. card from the Veterans Administration clinic, his Public Assistance cards, and a letter that his brother Steve had sent me from a prison out west after David died. And I read the journal and saw, clearly spelled out in my own hand, that I had indeed been in love with David. I was astonished that I began to sob as I read.

One passage was, it seemed, the seed out of which my dream had slowly and in secret grown through all those years. I'd written it in Hampton Bays on April 30th, 1990--nine days after David's death, and a few days before I'd buried his ashes there:

The hardest thing is that I'll never know for sure if he loved me, if he would have loved someone more under different circumstances, if I would have loved him less, or not at all, had he not been dying. I let him go, or he got away, before I could reconstruct his real life and understand all his lies about it. Two images hurt most; the first is one I made up: David 15 or 20 years ago, absolutely irresponsible and laughing about it, his arm out the window of a car on a Midwest highway on a hot day. Someone else is with him.

The other one is real: we're sitting on his bed in the afternoon after going out for a late breakfast. The T.V. is on and we've been laughing. After a few minutes of silence I can feel what's coming next, and he reaches over (not like him because he's shy), and puts his hand on my cheek and turns my face toward his, as if we could kiss and go from there. But we can't, and I'm afraid, and I only smile. The virus is between us, and it is

9

never going to go away, as much as we talk about cures and vaccines. I wish I had leaned over and really kissed him, if only that one time, but I held back, thinking that we would have more time.

No matter how bad he got, I always thought we had more time.

I was able to read only a little of the journal before I found it necessary to slam it shut and put it away, both because I didn't want my husband or son to see the effect it was having on me, and because it was so unexpectedly, unbearably painful to see what I'd written then. It was a few weeks, or perhaps months, until I was able to go back and read more.

When I did, and the memories of those eight months began to come back, I began not only to remember that I'd loved David, but also to see that losing him had changed who I was and who I might have become. And I remembered how badly I'd let him down at the very end, and how the hardest part of dealing with his death was knowing that I could never apologize to him, and that I would never get the chance to tell him that I loved him, or find out for certain if he loved me.

I remembered that I'd thought of myself at the time as an unacknowledged widow to a man I'd never married except in some hidden (even to him) place in my heart, with no right to grieve him properly. I remembered that I'd had to pretend that he was no different than any of the others, and that even the few people who knew what had happened between us saw it as a dangerous lapse, or an overabundance of misplaced compassion, and advised me to move on as quickly as possible. I remembered how alone we'd been, how circumspect we'd had to be, and how secretive. Perhaps the thing that I remembered most clearly was the constant sense that I was doing something wrong by being with him for those eight months, and the fact that I'd stayed with him anyway.

Professionalism, and the Pointlessness of Therapy

In one sense, it *was* wrong. He was my "client", and I was his "caseworker." In light of what we went through together in that shoddy little studio on the Lower East Side for the last eight months of David's life, those terms sound absurd. On the other hand, I knew perfectly well that it was expressly forbidden (although I'm quite certain that I was by no means alone in my transgression), and that I risked losing my job and possibly more by living with him as I did.

A therapist in whom I'd confided about my relationship with David at the time made the very astute comment that it was "unprofessional" (it was at that point that I came to regard therapists as utterly useless—I didn't need to pay someone to be told that it was unprofessional, and dangerous in a number of ways that had nothing to do with my physical health; what I needed was advice on how to survive the inevitable). The problem was that it became almost impossible for me to give a damn whether or not it was professional. Once I met him, nothing could have allowed me to let David spend the end of his life alone. Many, if not most, in his position did. At that time, in New York City, AIDS was like a wildfire, and those who were infected became—if they hadn't been already—outcasts, feared and despised, often disfigured by the easily recognized marks of the disease, rejected by the people who should have loved them regardless, evidence to the judgmental of God's wrath. I never had the courage to tell David that I loved him, but at least he knew that there was someone left who prayed that he would live, who wanted to sleep beside him at night, who would try to cool his fevers or keep him warm in winter, who would mourn him and bury him when the prayer went, inevitably, unanswered.

Knowing that, at least in retrospect, makes it easy to live with my utter lack of professionalism.

His Book

Before speaking became an effort too great to be made for anything beyond necessities like asking for some water to drink or help getting up from the bed, David asked me to write a book about him (as with many things, the unspoken remainder of his request would have been, "after I'm gone"). He had often seen me scribbling into my journal at night when I stayed at his apartment, and he was too intelligent, and knew me too well, to think that I wasn't writing about him sometimes. I didn't mean to make him self-conscious, but I suppose that some part of me knew that a concrete record of the details of was happening between us was something that I would need one day, if only to remember, once he was gone.

Still, I didn't write enough. There are many things that I left out, or made cryptic, incomplete notes about, not realizing that it would be sixteen years before I went back to try to decipher them in earnest, and that by then some of the memories might be all but completely faded. I was afraid that someone from work would find the journal, and that I might lose my job. And, at that point, I still believed that I was doing something wrong by loving David, and by trying to keep him happy and alive.

I like to think that he hoped that my writing his book would lead me, some day, to find his family and tell them about the man he was when I knew him—a man nothing like the one they remembered, or had heard about second-hand from other people who had seen only what he had presented to the world for most of his life. I don't remember if I promised him that I would; given my lackadaisical nature and my already well-established tendency to start things that I would never finish it would have been foolish to do so, but then I also had a tendency to do foolish things. In any case, I'd started to write a version of the story of our time together within a year after his death; I found the yellowed onionskin pages of what there was of it in the box where I'd found the old journal.

For years after that I'd tried in various other ways to honor David's request, but I never got far. I simply didn't know how to describe what had happened between us, and I think that I was also still feeling— even after all that time—that same sense of having done something wrong, something that no one else would ever possibly be able to understand. And there were still too many things that I didn't understand about him, and thought I never would.

Five or six years after David's death I wrote some poems about him; they were perhaps the most honest explorations of what we'd done and what I'd felt that I'd written so far, and perhaps they'd given me enough of a sense of that fictitious concept called "closure" at the time that I was able to put my nagging sense of neglected responsibility aside for the time-being and get on with the life that had somehow continued—blossomed even—almost in spite of me. The box was stored away, and I began to forget.

Ten years later I had the dream about the kiss, and the flood began.

******

David's book will be, in the end, a messy book, a book for which many of the usual rules don't work, a book that won't easily be defined as one thing or another---a book not unlike David himself. Over the years I've tried many times to find the right way to tell

15

the story, in all its layers of time, fact, fiction, emotion and understanding. I've tried to write it as a "conventional narrative", starting with the beginning and ending somewhere appropriate, but I've realized that there really was no discernible beginning (it could be said that it started many years before I ever met David, or, in some ways, years afterwards), and there will never, within my life, be an end. My perspective on what happened between us, and what happened before and after that time, will always be shifting and multi-faceted. Life, it seems to me now, is really like that—more of a gem than a timeline.

I've tried to write the story as "fiction", as a blog, as poetry, as a straight memoir. I've even thought about trying to write it as a screenplay, because so many of my memories are visual. But no one genre seems to be the "right" one.

I finally realized that the only way that feels right and natural is to take all of the bits and pieces—old journal entries, poems, pieces of the never-finished novel and memoir, blog posts, conversations I've had with David's family—that I've amassed over the last twenty-two years and put them together as organically as possible, in a way that makes sense to me. When something seems to require some explanation, I will explain it; if not, I will let it stand on its own. Each piece holds truth in one sense or another.

And David will finally, at least, have his book. One thing I remember well is that I always wanted to give him things that would make him happy.

PART TWO: EIGHT MONTHS

We called them "clients." The term struck me at the time as rather quaint—a demure attempt to allow them some sense that they were our partners in the journey that began with a diagnosis of full-blown AIDS, and not completely at our mercy. At any given time I had roughly thirty clients; some would die before I got a chance to meet them.

I'd taken the job as a caseworker for an agency created to provide financial and social services to those with full-blown AIDS in New York in 1988; I'd just turned 27. I had, so far, produced nothing that was worth much save a handful of pretty good poems. Having dabbled in some seriously risky behaviors myself during my college years and somewhat beyond (I'd been on the West Coast at the time; I believe that's what saved me), I didn't have it in me to look down on anyone who had not been so unreasonably lucky as I had been.

Somewhat confused sense of "wanting to help the less fortunate" aside, I'd also been in serious need of a job. I'd come very close to getting my Master's degree in Poetry a couple of years earlier, and had then focused my job-search, unsuccessfully, on a career in publishing, simply because I assumed that that was what one did if she'd been an English major. I'd always had a vague idea of "helping people" as a secondary career path, so when I answered the classified ad for a caseworker and, to my great surprise, got offered the job, I took it. (It was only later that I figured out that anyone who wanted the job and could hold herself more-or-less upright at a desk could be hired. The interview had basically consisted of one question—"Would you have any problem working with drug addicts or gay men?" I was simply fortunate in that I could honestly answer, "No.")

Most of the caseworkers in my office were gay, which made sense because gay people were pretty much the only people who gave a damn about people with AIDS back then (IV drug-users, presumably, gave a damn too, but they were, for the most part, less likely to be able to hold down a job for too long). Most of the other caseworkers were career civil service workers. They didn't particularly care if their clients were people with AIDS, serial killers, ballerinas, or rattlesnakes. A client was a client; it had a manila folder associated with it that needed to be dealt with. Once it was dealt with, the caseworker could go home and enjoy the evening. I'm not necessarily saying that they didn't care, but they had the "professional" thing down cold, and they did their jobs very well.

And then there was me.

******

All of the following entries were written in the year or so between the first week of my job at the agency and the day David first walked into my office. The ignorance and self-centeredness that some of them betray still appalls and shames me; in my own defense, however, we were all ignorant and afraid at that time.

2 October 1988
....So where was I? I'm happy with my little apartment on Adams Street, with my roommate Horacio (aside from the fact

that he seems to have been put off by Nick's staying here one weekend—he no longer considers me a "remarkable American," but I'd been trying to tell him that anyway), with the prospect of my AIDS job (which starts tomorrow, finally), with my friends and my apparent moderate, and inexplicable, notoriety in this weird tiny town full of people who refuse to ever grow up. I do love Hoboken, and I plan to for a while.

Just this morning (another inevitably gray Sunday), I feel a little lonely and anxious. I think I'm preparing for this job, testing each of my emotions to see if they're still working after a long period of dormancy. I've become a little worried that I can't feel passion any more, or at least that the opportunity might never come again...

4 October 1988

I keep thinking of myself as preparing to go into combat or on some expedition that will require the best physical and mental health. Well, it's true, really, I suppose. Apparently I'll be on call all the time and, although I'm not really afraid of getting AIDS, it occurred to me that these people are going to have all kinds of other contagious illnesses. "And that's one thing I don't wanna catch." So I have to get into condition again. Unfortunately, my hip prevents me from exercising very hard, and I'm still not very good at sitting alone and concentrating on things that will calm me and focus my mind—like writing and painting or just sitting. Reading's good, though...I read Carson McCuller's The Heart is a Lonely Hunter *in Florida, and was stunned at the beauty of her writing and her thought (it was published when she was 23, gnash, gnash). Now it's Kubler-Ross'* On Death and Dying—*much less impressive, but I thought it might help.*

6 October 1988

So immediately I get sick, and sit all day at our training session with a fever that makes me dizzy and clumsy. But I've been fighting it all day, and I feel better now. I know—I'm

19

beginning to sound like a health lunatic purist "precious bodily fluids" kind of individual, but I've finally got something to do for which I want to be at my best.

19 October 1988

Today I met my first "client," D. F. He just turned 30 and he's got "Wasting Syndrome," which means exactly what it sounds like it means. I was clumsy, but muddled through, and he was very sweet but, I think, exhausted by the questioning. The worst thing was having to ask him whether he had a burial fund. It was a horrible moment—he just looked at me for a few moments too long and then answered. I think he went back into the hospital this afternoon—I wonder if he'll come out.

(Strangely, "D.F.", in spite of his gauntness and apparent frailty, ended up living longer than almost any of my other clients—almost two years.)

2 January 1989

(This entry was about one of Margaret, a frail crack-addict who really—like so many of the others—wanted to be liked. I'd gotten her a room in an SRO hotel, and had gone shopping with her to buy some things for it, but shortly afterwards I'd found her in a bed at Harlem hospital, completely unresponsive. Someone had left a tray of food at the end of her bed, as if she were going to somehow rouse herself to sit up and eat it.)

She wouldn't blink. I was there for over an hour, trying to slap quick, persistent fruit flies away from her face, holding her hand and the metal bed-rail it was tied to, asking her to speak or to blink...Serene, irregular beep of a machine monitoring a woman's heart.

8 March 1989

In one apartment, a cat-'o'-nine-tails on a nail on the brick wall. A pile of stuffed bears next to the bed.

How are you feeling?

Oh, not too good. I've had this cold.

Have you seen a doctor?

I have an appointment tomorrow.

27 May 1989

At six the checks were still coming down. It was Friday, and there wasn't going to be much money to go around for the weekend for the clients whose checks didn't come. Some had been waiting weeks for late checks, living on the seven dollars they were given every night to take back to the hotels. Seven dollars or five and two tokens and occasionally a little extra out of the workers' pockets. Two women were crying, complaining in harsh whining junkie voices and smoking as if the cigarettes could nourish them.

11 March 1989

Grandma's in the hospital. A tumor on a bone made her arm break and she didn't realize it. They're doing tests on Monday, her birthday, so see if there are more tumors and, if so, whether they're malignant. I'm on the 4:59 Amtrak to Hartford, drinking a beer and thinking of a story.

18 July 1989

Grandma's back in the hospital. This time her hip's broken. It had been, apparently, somehow breaking slowly for a week before anyone took her to the hospital, ever since the car door hit her leg. They operated on Friday night, and they've found tumors all over her femur. We were waiting for her when they brought her back down to her room after the operation, and after putting her teeth back into her mouth she seemed the same as ever, only pretty giddy from the anesthesia. Grandpa asked her how it had gone, and she laughed and said, "Oh, I had a wonderful time!" No one else in the world...

The next day she was up in a chair, entertaining us, high on Demerol or Morphine. Once she asked me to get the nurse to put the oxygen tube back in her nose, very quietly and discreetly. Later, after having been brought to the bathroom, she was in pain again. I stood next to her bed and pulled the covers over her tiny shoulders and told her to close her eyes and just breathe slowly, which she did. I don't know if it helped. This sounds like sentimental bullshit, but I swear that if I could have changed places with her and taken on the pain I would have...For the past few months I guess I've had it in my head that I've gotten used to the idea of death, but when I think of her dying it seems that the ground will disappear under all of us. I suppose it's useless to think about how badly I treated her when I was unhappy, and about how much she always loved me anyway, but it's hard not to. When I do something good for someone now it seems to be somehow coming from her.

And then there's Grandpa. I've never seen him let anyone know that something could hurt him until now. He resists going to see Grandma, and often sleeps or sits and says nothing when we're with her, and it's easy to think that he doesn't understand what's going on. But he does. At the hospital he gets spacey and forgets things and people, but at home he's O.K. He tells stories about the trips he and Grandma have gone on, and jokes and sings songs, and people ignore him...I listen to him and ask questions. I wonder what he and Grandma say to each other when they're alone together. He says, "I guess this is the end. I just have a feeling." I honestly don't think I've ever seen two people more in love with each other.

My father had committed suicide when I was five, but he was not living with my mother and me at the time. Beyond that, I'd had almost no experience with death, or the anticipation of a death, up until that point in my life.

The Walk-In

I'd been doing my job very badly for almost a year (a combination of having zero organizational skills, a succession of hangovers caused by staying out too late at the local clubs and bars in Hoboken, where I lived, and a series of preoccupations with a string of boyfriends whom I'd met at the aforementioned clubs and bars) on the day David walked in. That's what he was–"a walk-in client"—someone who'd just heard about us somewhere and wandered in off the street to see if there was any way we could help, or who'd been sent over by one of the hospitals. (Other clients just showed up as manila folders, which contained everything we needed to know about what they didn't have, along with descriptions of their mental and rapidly deteriorating physical states, on our desks. As I said earlier, some of them didn't even live long enough for me to make my first visit to their apartments or hospital rooms.)

It was late in the day; I'd no doubt recently returned from one of the long lunches that my coworkers and I often indulged in together, drinking strong cocktails and sharing stories about our clients and our romances-of-the-moment. It had been raining most of the day—the kind of rain that seems like continuous, dispirited spitting from some bored god. The office had no windows, but a yellow-grey dampness seemed to be coming in from somewhere, or trailing in behind the clients as they entered the building. At least that's how I remember it.

I have a picture of David that was taken that day—August 8th, 1989--for his Public Assistance I.D. card. (I also have a second P.A. card, dated two weeks later, as well as a Handicap I.D. card for the buses and subways, a V.A. Hospital clinic card, a V.A. Patient Data card, a Medicaid card, and, oddly enough, a voter registration card. If you were poor and sick back then, your cards were everything.) In the picture, he looks exactly as I remember him that day, and as anyone who had been living on the street for a week or so would look—wet, exhausted, feverish perhaps, possibly in withdrawal, too worn-out to hold his head up straight or his mouth properly shut. His hair, black with streaks of gray, is especially curly from the dampness outside, and there are bags under his eyes. (One of the few things I clearly remember about that day is that I couldn't stop looking at his eyes, which were dark brown, with elaborately rounded upper lids that sloped sharply down toward the outer edges. I thought that they were beautiful.). The expression on his face is one of someone who has been beaten without mercy, and is looking at the end into the eyes of his tormentor to see if there's more coming. He looks, in short, like someone whom many people would cross the street to avoid.

I remember feeling for the first couple of minutes after we shook hands and he sat down that he might be one of the few clients who would give me some trouble. There was something defiant, and a little angry, about him—not rude at all, but wary, and clearly not happy about having to defer to a stranger in order to get a safe place to sleep, some money in his pocket, and medical care. Who would be, after all? My impression was that he'd been accustomed to getting what he needed for himself, by whatever means necessary. Being too sick to do so was a new experience for him, and he meant to let me know that. But that cloud passed almost immediately, and I never saw it again after that day. Any "trouble" he gave me turned out to be of a very different sort, and I would gladly take it on again.

That afternoon, we sat at my desk and had a much longer conversation than any client/caseworker interview would warrant. To be honest, there's very little that I remember of the specifics of what David said that day, or of many of the more trivial things that we used to talk about, or that made us laugh together, in the months afterward. I vaguely remember his saying something about an ex-wife, and having lived in or traveled to more states than I would have believed possible, and having fought in Vietnam. The thing that struck me the most, however, was his pride in having Chippewa blood, and in having lived on one of the reservations in Minnesota.

What I don't remember is if I doubted any of his story, but I know that I had a tendency to feel that it would be rude not to believe the stories (and I heard a lot of them) that people told me about their lives. As it turned out, I'd have the next seventeen years of my life to wonder what was true, and what David simply wanted to believe about himself, and what just made a good story.

We talked until it was past time for me to go home. I walked out of the building with him, out into the rain and the prematurely dark chaos of Fourteenth Street. I bought him a hot dog, a cheap umbrella from a street vendor, and a bunch of bananas, before we went our separate ways—he to an SRO hotel on 106th Street, where I'd arranged for him to stay until we could find him something more permanent, and I back to my apartment in Hoboken and, no doubt, another night out.

I think I already knew what would happen, even if I didn't acknowledge it to myself at the time.

Beast and Prey

"Simon" was one of several pseudonyms I gave David in my various attempts to write about him. This is an excerpt from an early attempt to write a novel about him:

Four blocks down First Avenue from Bellevue, Simon turned to look back and everything exploded and began to burn. Windows framed fires that wavered with contained fury against black brick and stone. Rockets arced up, hissing and whistling, over the river, bloomed fast, hung for a moment in the milky, acrid air, and fell, burning out and disappearing halfway down. Headlights bounced and veered toward him. Heat rose from the sidewalk and from a point between his eyes, and after lifting his arm to shield his face he became calm and walked for hours.

At 3:30 the police found him sitting naked in a doorway on Rivington Street and brought him back to the hospital. At the admitting desk he remembered who he was, but nothing of the night. His temperature was 103 degrees, and his lungs were full of fluid.

That day and night and the night after Simon sweated and gasped and hallucinated in Intensive Care. During the worst of it his hands had to be tied to the bedrails so that he wouldn't pull the oxygen tubes out of his nose or dig his fingernails into the old scars on the backs of his hands. A few times he became lucid and cool and spoke to the nurse about how he felt, but he never mentioned what the doctor had told him just before he left the hospital and blacked out, and no one brought it up.

By the beginning of the third day Simon no longer needed to be in Intensive Care. He was taken down to the regular HIV ward on a cart, covered with a stiff sheet. He felt drained and dry and weightless, wrecked and burned clean, like driftwood. His ears were full of flat tones and surf sounds. During the day he fanned flies away from his face, and watched the light flatten and fade on the white walls, then become warm and orange as beach light toward evening. He drank his methadone but was unable to eat anything but a little rice at lunch, and some pudding at dinner.

That night he dozed, dreaming over and over that he'd stopped dreaming and gotten out of bed to watch the lights of boats moving slowly on the East River. Then he'd wake for a few moments, realize he'd still been dreaming, and start over. The lights and the dark room looked the same in his dreams as they did when he was awake.

David—like many others who, at that time, were given an AIDS diagnosis—tried at first to deny it, outrun it, just forget and go on. What didn't—like many things—occur to me then was that he, having been "raised" (and I use the term advisedly) by people who considered themselves religious, must have at that moment clearly seen hell just ahead of him, panting like some wild animal that had lain silently in wait for him and was finally about to take its prey.

I wish that I had understood that about him, and about so many of the others, then. Although it was natural, at first, to try to deny the reality that there really was no hope, and to at least think about putting up some kind of a fight, an AIDS diagnosis at that time washed away that sense of immortality, freedom from the judgments of the past, and limitless possibility that being a young person (and, with very few exceptions, they were all young) in New York City provided. Once that insulation was stripped away they were often thrown right back on the parsimonious mercy of the religious and social values they'd come so far to escape. I was deeply saddened, for example, when one of my clients—a beautiful, intelligent, sweet, successful gay man who worked as a model and had been raised in the South by strict Baptists—called me at the very end to tell me that he had gone home, that he had been wrong, and that all

27

he wanted was his family's forgiveness and love, to which he would not be entitled unless he became someone other than the man he really was.

As for David, I don't know what he would have even been able to consider "home" at that point. I'm not sure, in fact, that he ever knew where that might be.

The Puppy

About two weeks after I met him, David had to come in to the office again to get his picture taken for a card that identified him as a disabled person, so that he could pay half-fare on the subways and buses. For some reason, he also needed to get a new picture for a new Public Assistance I.D. card. The difference in his appearance in those pictures, and the one taken on the day I met him, is remarkable. In the later pictures, it's obvious that he'd shaved, trimmed his mustache, and brushed his hair back neatly, and he looks rested and healthy and handsome. The picture on the new P.A. card looks a little like a mug shot (although, when I had it enlarged years later, I noticed that there is an all-but-imperceptible smile on his lips), but in the Transit photo he's looking down, with a slight, wistful smile that makes him look as if he's remembering a sweet secret. I wish I knew what it was that he was thinking about; it's nice to entertain the unlikely possibility that he might have been thinking of me. It's not as if he had much else to smile about at that point.

I must have thought about him a great deal during those first few weeks, no doubt telling myself that it was only because there was something fascinating in his story and in the way he told it, and in his dark eyes. I know that I looked forward to seeing him again.

At that time, I'd decided to adopt a puppy from the ASPCA. David came into the office on the day I planned to make the trip uptown to pick out the puppy. I remember thinking as we talked that it might be nice for him to come along instead of spending the rest of the afternoon in the SRO with nothing to do (at least that's how I was attempting to justify it to myself), and feeling shy about asking him. Something told me that, in spite of the commonly held notion that heroin addicts have no interest in anything other than getting high, it would be something that he would enjoy. I have an image in my mind of my running (as if it had been an afterthought) to catch up with him as he started to leave the office, and of asking him in some nervous, almost apologetic jumble of words. And I remember the sweet, surprised look on his face when he said yes.

I don't remember the ride uptown, or looking at the puppies, but I think that I can see us sitting together in the office at the ASPCA as if we were a couple, answering questions, adopting the puppy together.

It must have been early evening by the time we left the ASPCA. The hotel that David was staying at was across town and a few blocks up from the ASPCA; I had to go back downtown in order to get back to Hoboken. We took the cross-town bus to the west side together, both of us peering into the box that held the puppy, who was a shepherd/lab mix, and petting his sleek little black head, murmuring affectionate gibberish, before we parted for the night. I gave David some money to get himself a decent dinner somewhere (he hadn't asked for it; he never asked), no doubt wishing that I could have gone with him but also looking forward to taking my puppy home.

David suggested that I name the puppy Sammy, and I did. Years later, I found out that "Sam" had been an alias that David had used on the street in New York, and I wondered what had made him suggest it for what I think I considered, without really acknowledging it then, "our" dog.

30

The Apartment, and a Long Walk Downtown

There are no entries in my journal for that September. I do know that, at some point late in the month, David and I set about finding him an apartment of his own. (There was nothing unusual in this; the City of New York required that anyone with full-blown AIDS be given, at the City's expense, permanent housing when possible, and immediate housing in an SRO hotel until something better could be found. No one was left to spend a single night on the street, or in a shelter. You have to give them credit—things didn't always work smoothly, checks came late, and mistakes got made, especially on my cases. For the 1980's, though, it was a pretty enlightened, and compassionate, concept.) David had told me that he had some friends who owned a few buildings on the Lower East Side, and who might help him out for old times' sake by renting him an apartment that met the City's rent requirement (about $680 per month at the time, as I recall, although they could often be persuaded to pay a little more).

The friends, David said, knew him from his days as a carpenter. I vaguely remember them as a sweet, middle-aged couple, who seemed genuinely fond of David. They weren't so great at building maintenance, but they did what they could for David, and that was enough for me.

One of my earliest attempts to write David's book for him included this account of the day we arranged to rent his apartment on Suffolk Street (here, David was "Sam" and I was "Anne"):

The neighborhood that he brought her to was a neighborhood of gravestones, but he didn't seem to notice and she didn't mention it. A friend—someone he said he used to work for—

had an apartment there that he might rent to Sam for a sum that Welfare would consider reasonable. It was on a street just off the east side of Houston, where deserted buildings tipped at various angles like dominoes about to fall.

Later, to a friend, Anne referred to it as the Memorial District. On every block there was at least one showroom full of polished markers, some blank and some already engraved with names, and with coiling tendrils and blossoms. She noticed, as she always had at cemeteries, the disparities in size and workmanship and ornateness of the stones, and wondered at how the dead's stature in life could seem to be reflected by a piece of granite. It would be better if the body vanished with the last exhalation of breath, the final jolt and halting of the heart.

She wished that Sam would look for a place in another part of town, but he felt comfortable on the Lower East Side and said that he had a lot of friends there who would help him if he got really sick. Besides, cheap apartments were hard to come by, and landlords weren't usually anxious to rent to people on Welfare. Sam was in no position to consider Anne's omens.

And he'd tired of the hotel, of the junkies and crackheads banging on his doors at all hours of the night and day to try to make a sale (he said he hadn't been buying; she took his word for it) or get a cigarette or just talk wild coke-talk, of the window that wouldn't close all the way, of the filth of the shared bathrooms in the hallway. Sam had become finicky about cleanliness in a way he said he never was before. He now believed that it was his key to staying alive.

At that time, on many days, he really thought he'd beat the thing. He said it that day, as they were crossing Houston to Suffolk Street.

"I don't know," he said, lightly touching her arm for a moment as if to guide her up the curb onto the sidewalk (she wondered where he'd learned to perform those small chivalrous gestures with such natural grace that she sometimes felt clumsy beside him). "I get a feeling I'll make it. Everyone is working on a cure, right? Like that one thing you told me about. That could be it, right?"

There were many things that could be it, each whispered about or exulted over in the newsletters for weeks or months until reports of side-effects, pancreas damage or anemia or death, or of something else that held more promise, began to appear. At the time Anne couldn't even remember which one she'd mentioned, but she was vulnerable to hope too—especially, by that time and for reasons she hadn't allowed herself to think about, for his sake. So she nodded and said, "Could be," and let it go, with superstitious forbearance, at that.

It was just warm enough that day to walk coatless, as long as they stayed out of the shade. Farther downtown, toward the World Trade Center, there seemed to be a sun slipping down behind every building. Early for the appointment, Sam and Anne walked the streets around the apartment building in a gradually shrinking circle until they were across the street from it. There they waited, watching for the super. Sam pulled a milk-crate out into the sunlight so that Anne could sit. To pass time, and as if he was afraid that she'd get bored and leave, Sam pointed out buildings whose facades he'd painted, whose plumbing he'd installed, whose basements he'd cleared of debris.

"I had a crew of eight men under me," he was saying. "The neighborhood didn't look the same after we came through, boy. I was making damn good money, too. My arms were as big as trees."

She asked him, "Wasn't it hard to work when you were high?"

"No. I was making good money then. I'd have everything ready in the morning and pop it right in on my way out the door. Just like that. No damn doctor can hit a vein like I can."

"Like picking up a briefcase."

"I guess. Yeah. I wasn't fucked up then. When you've got the money coming in, it's no problem."

33

"So what happened?"

"Something's always going to give on you."

Up the street a VW pulled up to the curb and two young men in Oxford shirts and blue jeans got out. They walked quickly up the street. Sam looked disgusted.

"Weekend warriors," he said. "College boys. Come down here to cop and bring it uptown to their friends. Think they're hot shit." He flicked his cigarette in their general direction. "Damn fools."

The super, who was the son of Sam's friends and knew Sam too, came thirty-five minutes late, but made no apology. His greeting was reserved, a little suspicious, and nowhere near as warm as Sam's. If Sam noticed, he didn't show it. Anne unwillingly felt a little embarrassed for him, because his eagerness to let her know that he'd had friends and something of a life besides drugs before he got sick was so evident, and because this clod with the keys in his hand couldn't see that and help him out a little. She found herself defending Sam by making as much of a show of affection and respect for him as she could get away with without seeming unprofessional.

Before going inside to see the place they had a lengthy discussion about the rent, which, Anne assured the clod (whose name was Mel), would be guaranteed by Welfare. She told him that it would just be a matter of days (it was best, when dealing with Welfare, to be as unspecific as possible about those things) until he saw some money. Sam stood with his hands in his pockets, his feet moving restlessly as they talked. Every so often he would back up what she was saying with an excited, "She's right, Mel—she knows what she's talking about. You can trust her."

Mel was eventually convinced, and they finally went inside. The hallway smelled of seasoned rice and chicken frying and mildew, and seemed colder than it was outside. There was rust-red linoleum on the floor, but much of it had curled back or disintegrated to reveal the even more ancient floor beneath it, a mosaic of tiny white and black tiles.

34

"This be the place," Mel said, now affecting an air of joviality unsuited to him. He was standing in front of a black door at the top of a flight of stairs that led down into complete darkness. There was only one other door in the hallway, and there was a sound of wind whistling through the crack at its bottom, as if there were a window open inside.

Mel unlocked the upper and lower locks to the apartment and opened the door, standing aside to let Sam and Anne go in first.

There wasn't much to the place; it was a medium-sized studio divided by some appliances and a trick of the imagination into a kitchen and living area. Next to the kitchen sink was an enormous old bathtub, and the toilet was in a closet-sized room at the front of the apartment. The walls were white, the sloping wood floors painted gray. Two large, barred windows at the back looked out onto a yard full of scrap metal and old refrigerators, and a burned-out building.

Sam walked in circles, too excited to stop and look at anything. Anne opened the refrigerator ("Brand-new," said Mel), flushed the toilet, ran the faucets, lit the stove. Everything worked. The windows, she was thinking, were what saved the place from being a cave. They'd let in a lot of warm sunlight, at least in the morning, and in summer there might be enough of a breeze to keep it cool. She went to stand at one and look outside. Sam came over next to her and whispered, in the tone of a child praising the virtues of some toy to his mother without daring to come out and ask for it, "Not bad, huh?"

"Not bad," she answered. "But we'll have to clean it." She hadn't meant to include herself.

"Oh, we can clean it." Sam took her answer as approval, and started making plans. "I'll get a T.V. over here, and one of those beds you can fold up into a couch that way by the window, and a couple of chairs around the place. We can fix it up into a nice place."

Anne was feeling confused and anxious about her role in all of this now. She turned to Mel, who'd been standing with feigned disinterest in the kitchen. "How's the heat?" she asked.

"Plenty of heat. No complaints."

They spent a few minutes working out the final details of the agreement, and by the time they got outside it was getting dark, and cold. Buildings looked pale and phosphorescent against the sky, as if they had soaked up light all day and were reluctant to give it up to the night air.

Sam took a long time saying goodbye to and thanking Mel, who had warmed up considerably to the prospect of having a new tenant. As they reminisced about the neighborhood Anne stood outside the high metal fence of the lot next to Sam's building. Inside were more gravestones. Toward the back of the lot was a big granite angel, unfinished, its features pitted and ghastly in the shadows. An obsessive evaluator of omens, Anne didn't know whether to think of it as a good or a bad one, or as nothing at all.

Afterwards, David was exuberant about the prospect of having a home of his own; it had been a long time since he'd lived anywhere but on the street or in some lousy hotel. He talked and talked, making plans for the apartment and telling me more stories about the neighborhood and his life before he got sick. We walked south, then west, then south again; we crossed Seward Park, but cautiously. There were people David didn't want to see. When we reached the other side of the park David told me that when he got tested for TB the nurse did it twice, sticking him once on each arm. He believed that that was how he got it—being jabbed twice. They weren't that careful with people like him, he told me. I said that I didn't know much about it. "I do," he said.

It was well past time for me to go home, but something compelled me to keep walking with him farther and farther downtown, listening, fascinated, and well aware that I was once again toeing the increasingly indistinct line between client and caseworker. Every so often I'd stop and tell him that I really had to get back to Hoboken. "Just one more block," he'd say, and that would be enough to keep me going (he was never pushy, but he could be very convincing when he wanted or needed to be). It finally became clear that I wouldn't be turning back—that I'd be spending the evening with David, that I wanted to spend it with him. I stopped resisting, and I suppose that was when I knew that the line had actually already been crossed.

We had supper at a Chinese place whose owner liked David (it was again clear that David wanted to show me that there were people who liked and trusted him) and had often given him a meal when he was on the street, and then we walked some more. David wanted to leave the man an enormous tip—something to cover all the tips he hadn't been able to leave before, and he wanted to treat me to dinner. I don't think I let him.

It had been dark for a while when we ended the night having *tiramisu* and coffee, and probably some anisette, at least for me (David really didn't drink), at a café in Little Italy. I don't remember what we talked about, but there seemed to be a lot to say, and it felt very easy being with him, as if we'd known each other for a long time. David, actually, did most of the talking, as if he hadn't had anyone to tell his stories to for quite a while. But I was content to listen.

We finally parted for the night at a subway station on Houston. I remember turning to see him standing there in the dark, watching me again with that sweet, surprised look on his face, and I remember having the conscious thought that I was in trouble.

37

One of the poems I wrote about David in the mid-'90's was also about that day:

SEWARD PARK

Longer than I thought, the walk
Across Houston, through Seward Park
To a part of Chinatown I'd never seen.
It was September. Blue milk spilled from sky
To street, and lights were sparking on.
I don't remember where
We meant to go, or who was leading whom.

Tarnished sea bass gasped in window tanks,
Slid their bellies in nervous shimmies up
The glass, losing scales, mouthing
Breathless O's, then flipped
Back into the crowded dark,
To let the others have a go.

I watched you eat
And paid for it
In a restaurant where in the windows
Ducks hung by their necks on hooks, plucked,
All flesh, eyeless heads bent sideways
In attitudes of shame.
By the time you finished, it was dark.
Leaves under streetlamps fanned from branches
Over shadows splayed and swaying, cards
Held in a nervous hand. I meant to leave you then,
But you were talking
And I had no one at home.

The Street

There's another chapter from my first attempt at writing David's book that, having been written soon enough after his death that the memories hadn't had a chance to fade yet, is a very telling—although obviously slightly fictionalized in terms of timing and some of the circumstances—account of who he was and what he was doing just before we met, and of my state of mind shortly after losing him. It begins with a contemplation of a photograph I had of him (blown up from the picture I'd peeled off of one of his I.D. cards after his death), and then moves back in time to a memory of something he told me:

...The image is a little vague, a little eerie. The enlarging process does that. I bought a frame and pressed some dried flowers from Assateague between the picture and the glass, and set it up on the table beside my bed. His eyes follow me around the room, and when I look back into them the ghost, the flimsy cloud, emerges from the darkness around it, hardening into something I can recognize more easily as him.

It's hard to look at that face, that particular expression, as a single image. The eyes, with their look of asking for something with no expectation of the wish being granted, have nothing to do with the mouth, which the camera seems to have caught just as Sam thought of something else, went out west or downtown in his head, and let the corners of his mouth slip down out of a smile. There is a tension only just above his eyebrows, which are slightly lifted. Above them is the smooth forehead, and it's easy to remember how it felt to push his hair up a little with my hand and feel for the fever that always seemed to be there.

It was that expression that he wore the day he found me again in my office after spending the night in the Fourteenth Street subway station. The picture was actually taken on that day when I took him over to Welfare for an emergency check, a hotel room, and permission to look for a place of his own to live. After we got him some methadone as a "courtesy" from the hospital clinic, and arranged for him to keep coming, I took him to a coffee shop on Sixth Avenue to get a sandwich. The muscles in his throat and jaw were so sore from shivering that he found it hard to eat, hungry as he was.

Certain details of the day I remember: rain like needles flung against the window next to the booth where we were sitting, the sky gray, the air yellow. His brown flannel shirt torn at the sleeve, and the delicate way he held the spoon when he stirred milk and four spoonfuls of sugar into his coffee. Once he got some food down he started to revive like a dry plant given water. Giddy from the nourishment, and from the methadone kicking in, he started to tell me about the night.

I remember the illustrations my mind provided for the story better than what he actually said: the elevator door at the hospital opening onto a lobby softly lit and decorous as a funeral parlor, the walls and upholstery the colors of fresh and dried blood. A man and a little boy sitting on a sofa in one corner (Sam remembered because the man looked a little like his foster-father, and it seemed strange to him that a boy would sit so close to him), and track-lighting above them, creating shadows that disfigured their faces.

There is an arch for detecting metal near the doors, and a security guard (handsome, quite young, black—I remember him and his sweet, slightly flirtatious jokes from the times I visited David in the hospital later) was leaning against the wall near it. He was watching the screen of the T.V. that hangs from the ceiling, and he paid no attention to Sam, who felt bad for a moment that no one noticed his walking out. The feeling, Sam said, passed.

I know the route he took very well: the automatic doors opening smoothly and very wide, with a reassuring mechanical hum and a rush of air from outside, as Sam's feet touched the rubber mat in front of it. Outside, moths would have been circling each other under the floodlights, creating a little

40

snowstorm through which, once his eyes adjusted, he'd be able to see the section of Twenty-third Street east of First Avenue, deserted except for a few taxis speeding toward and away from the river.

"There was nothing to do except start walking," he said. "Right away the sweat started pouring down my back, and I could hardly see in front of me with the goddamn headlights coming up at me."

But he kept going, squinting or looking down at the sidewalk as he went, staying as close to the thick, placid-looking buildings of Peter Cooper Village as he could. There are cobblestones under the young elms planted along the outer edges of the complex, and I laughed when he told me that he tried to step only on the smooth ones, because I used to do the same thing when I was a child, growing up in Peter Cooper. He said he felt small and slow, as he did in dreams in which he tried to run and couldn't, and every few steps he turned to look over his shoulder.

For the first few blocks he thought that he could feel a warm tingling on his back coming from the direction of the hospital, as if there were some kind of invisible connection between him and it, pulling harder and threatening to snap like an elastic band as he moved farther away. But he forgot about it by the time he reached Fourteenth Street, where everything seems to move much faster and the lights on summer nights sizzle from their own heat.

He turned east toward Avenue A. Girls and young men stood in the darker spaces between the bodegas and pizza parlors and newsstands muttering, "Smoke, smoke," but he didn't look at them. He was wondering how he'd get his methadone in the morning, and whether his friend Lenny would still be awake. (I learned later that it was hard to predict these things with Lenny, who was by turns a narcoleptic and an insomniac.)

By the time Sam reached 11th and A, Lenny's block, he was having trouble breathing. His chest hurt where there were holes

41

in his lungs, but he was afraid to stop and rest because he might miss Lenny and be out for the night.

"I used to like to sleep outside," he told me, a little angrily. "But I wasn't up to it last night. Look at me. I looked alright yesterday."

He told me then about Lenny and the building. Lenny had bought it in 1964, the year his daughter Susan was born. It was nothing but a burned-out and slightly sagging wreck by then, but Lenny had a plan for it and he spent the next 25 years in his drowsy and directionless way to make it livable.

"He was always taking bums in off the street to work with him on it. Half of them would do a half-ass job for a couple of days, grab some money off of Lenny, and disappear. Not me. I got the plumbing finished and got the place into shape for him. He loved me, boy. And he took care of me. Lenny's the only person in the world I trust. Completely."

Lenny's original idea had been to finish the building by Susan's 21st birthday and give it to her then, but his health, and a series of misfortunes about which I later heard him speak in a rambling and resigned way over dinner at the Polish restaurant on 6th Street, had put him several years behind schedule. Sam believed that Susan, who lived far out in New Jersey with her second husband and two children, had no interest in the building, but he never said anything because Lenny had very little in his life except for his daughter and his building. His wife had left him years ago, finally tiring of the sawdust and unfinished walls with silver- and salmon-colored insulation exposed, and the noise of hammering and sawing and drilling.

Lenny's lights were on, but that didn't mean much because when he fell asleep there was no preparation. He just stopped. There was a buzzer outside, but the wires had never been connected and there was no way to get inside except by yelling upstairs until Lenny heard and either came down or dropped the keys, wrapped in a sock, down to the street.

42

Sam said that by then his calves felt like twitching rubber bands and when he breathed in there was a wheezing noise that sounded as if it were coming from somewhere outside of him. He put his hands around his mouth and called for Lenny, but the name came out shallow and high, and again he felt as if he was dreaming, unable to make himself heard to save his life. There was no response. He yelled again, but as he did a car passed behind him and drowned out the small sound he made. His legs were really shaking now, threatening to crumple under him. After another car had passed he sucked air as far down inside of his lungs as it would go and tried again: "Lenny. Lenny, it's Sam. Wake the fuck up." That time he did it loud enough to be heard, but Lenny didn't come.

He went to the door and tried to turn the knob, but as he did he could hear in his mind how it always clicked and locked by itself after it shut. Besides, there was a chain and another lock inside; Lenny always used them.

"He's hard to figure," Sam told me, grinning. "You'd think he wouldn't remember how to breathe half the time, but then when it comes to keeping his building safe he's crafty as a cockroach."

Sam's legs gave out and he sat down with his back against the door. People passed but no one looked at him. A fever was starting (first chills coming up from the ground through the legs, and then a parched, aching feeling in the bones and muscles and face), and his empty stomach began to pant inside of him, threatening nausea.

"I knew I wouldn't make it back to the hospital," he said. "And if I did I'd be up all night trying to explain what was what to the doctors. They might not have even let me back in. No. They'd have to, I guess. All I wanted to do was find a place to lay my head down, and 25 dollars to get myself some methadone in the morning."

He leaned his head back against Lenny's door and looked up at the sky. (No stars, but a milky film hanging just below the black, reflecting and distorting the lights from the streets,

43

threatening rain or chilly dampness later.) The fever was making him shiver. He closed his eyes, pulled his knees up as close as they would go to his chest, crossed his arms all the way around him like a lover's arms, and prayed that he'd be lucky enough to fall asleep and wake up alive in the morning. There was a small chance that Lenny would come down later to take one of his insomniac strolls around the block.

After a while he did sleep, but he was nervous and getting sicker, and his mind didn't quite let go of the fact that he was sleeping on a doorstep. ("Like a bear with no teeth and his balls cut off," he said. "Excuse me.") His dreams were sickly extensions of his waking thoughts, and every few minutes he'd twitch and wake up. At one point he thought he saw Lenny coming down the block, and he could hear his heavy, impossibly slow footsteps and the jingle of his keys. Just as he raised his hand to have Lenny help him up he woke up completely, having hit his hand on the rough brick wall next to him. Someone was pissing into the street in front of the building. Sam's shirt was wet, and his shivering was uncontrollable now. He measured his sleeping time against real time, and knew that hardly any time had passed at all.

The shaking had made all of his muscles cramp up, and when he stood the pain made him groan. He looked up again at Lenny's windows. The lights were out now. That meant that Lenny had been up, but had gone to bed in the back of the apartment. It meant that there was no hope.

Swaying, he looked up toward First Avenue and then back down toward Tompkins Square Park. He had to get inside somewhere and get some sleep so that he'd have the strength to get himself set up in the morning. There was a shelter on 3rd Street, but even if he had a chance in hell of talking someone into letting him in this late he'd be up all night with cockroaches crawling on his face and crackheads and thieves roaming among the cots, looking for something they could sell or keep. The hospital, he told me, had spoiled him for all of the things he could have put up with as a junkie.

44

There was a bandshell in the park, but by then Sam knew that he had to be inside somewhere, safe and unmolested so that he could really sleep. It occurred to him that the subway station on Fourteenth and First was his best bet. It would be warm and if anyone bothered him it would probably be a cop, giving him a wake-up call by beating a nightstick on the wall next to his head. He could stretch out on one of the benches at the back of the station. And if there was a problem he could just jump on the L train and ride all night.

First Avenue looked warmer and brighter, somehow, than Avenue A, so he went that way, stopping often, his arms crossed around him so that the chills wouldn't split his chest open. Passing NYU kids dressed up as bikers or junkies or punks, or young bankers downtown to drink and see the sights, all traveling in confused packs in and out of the little Polish-run bars and restaurants, he noticed that most ignored him or gave him a quick up-and-down look.

"Like I just crawled out of a manhole looking for money or drugs," he put it. It made him feel safer to know that they were more afraid of him than he was of them—that they couldn't see his weakness.

By the time he made it to the subway entrance he thought that he might die before he got downstairs. He was exhausted and sick to his stomach from shivering and not eating, and his chest felt like there was a fire inside. His legs were numb, and as he hung on to the banister and put one foot after the other down the stairs it was as if he was walking on crooked stilts.

The air inside the station was so thick and hot that it seemed he could grab a handful of it. There was no one down there except for a token-booth clerk, counting money.

This was the last obstacle. Sam went to the window of the booth, trying to look as earnest and respectable as he could, and waited until the clerk had finished counting the wad of ones in her hand. Eventually she looked up at him, expressionless.

"Hi," he said. She lifted her chin a little. He smiled in his gentlest way (the eyes in the photograph, only a little more

45

desperate, more calculating). "I was wondering if you could help me. I'm sick and I lost my wallet and I have to get across town or my wife is really going to worry. Can you just let me through the gate and I promise..."

"You got to pay your fare," said the clerk, clearly, with a rhythm she obviously used to say the same thing a hundred times a day.

"I just told you, I don't have my..."

"I just told YOU, you got to pay your fare."

"Look, please just give me a break. I'm really sick. I can't walk any more."

"Pay your fare." She went back to counting her money.

Sam felt that he might cry. He'd been arrested once for jumping a turnstile, and he'd spent the night in a bullpen so crowded that he couldn't sit down, and stinking so much of piss that he didn't want to. At the time, having been locked up once or twice before, he'd taken it pretty much in stride; that night he thought it might kill him. He started to walk back over to the stairs, just to sit, but someone was coming down. It was a teenage girl. He considered asking her for a token but he was afraid that the only thing that would come out would be a whine or a sob. The girl went to the token booth.

"Fuck it," Sam whispered to himself, and he turned and quickly ducked under one of the turnstiles to the other side.

Behind him he heard, "Pay your fare, sir," but he ignored it and walked to a bench at the end of the platform. The station smelled almost as bad as the bullpen but he didn't care because he was going to sleep. He cleared some pages of the Post *off of the bench, took his shirt off and made a pillow out of it, and lay down. He slept, as he put it, like a dead man.*

There the memory ends, not with the image of Sam sitting across the table from me, reciting his story with the attention to detail of a man to whom nothing has happened in a long time, but with that last one, the picture that my mind supplied as illustration: Sam, viewed from a point far up the subway platform, curled, oblivious and half-naked, mouth slightly open

46

and hair clinging to his damp, smooth forehead, on the bench nearest to where the track goes dark and curves away.

I know why I put so much into the description of Lenny. I remember the night I met him, in his construction-site of a building, and I remember sitting next to David at one of the Polish coffeeshops a little later, listening to him and Lenny talk about the work they'd done together. I remember being a little uncomfortable, like a girl being introduced to her boyfriend's father (and, at that point, I still hadn't allowed myself to think of our relationship in those terms). And I remember how eager David seemed for me to understand that Lenny really cared about him, and respected him and the work he was capable of doing.

But I don't think I realized at the time how close my sense of the situation came to the truth. It wasn't until sixteen years later that I realized just how fatherless David had always been, and that Lenny may have come closer to playing that role in his life than anyone else ever had.

Steps

There are no journal entries about what happened in the few weeks following our walk through downtown Manhattan, and how my life gradually became hopelessly intertwined with David's. I'm sure that it happened the way all forays into the forbidden seem to happen—a series of small, seemingly unremarkable events, each a little closer to an inevitability that seems inevitable only in retrospect, steps down a long road whose descent is so gradual that you don't notice that you're walking downhill. I know that I helped him, with money provided to him by the city for that purpose (probably supplemented by a little of my own), buy a few things for the apartment in the discount stores on Fourteenth Street or on the Lower East Side—plates, silverware, a futon mattress and sheets and pillows for it. We would have shopped for some groceries, and I might have stopped by with something I knew he needed on my way home from work. One night I would have cooked him a meal because he was too tired to cook anything decent for himself, and on another night I would have done it again, staying a little later each time.

A Kind of Love

There's a chapter of the book I tried to write that provides what is probably a pretty accurate account of what I was feeling at the time, incorporating memories that were still fairly fresh. In it, I had just moved into a new apartment of my own after having lived for a year or so with a roommate, whose name was Joe:

There was too much of everything: too much space, too much heat, too many boxes lining the walls, filled with things she could barely remember having owned. A mattress on the floor covered with too many blankets and four pillows. Three bottles of wine in the refrigerator and one, open and half-empty, on the floor beside her. A bowl of fruit going black and soft before she had the chance to eat it. There was so much potential around her that it paralyzed her, or started her dreaming about where she'd be next. It had crossed her mind that maybe there was too little of her.

She should have settled in by now. It had been three weeks since Joe had dropped her off there with the boxes and the housewarming gifts of wine and fruit and the forsythia branches that he'd picked up in the Flower District early in the morning while she was still asleep. But every time she thought of putting something on a shelf or in a corner or closet she started to think about all the other places it could be, sometimes going so far as to imagine that on the day she moved from this apartment into another she would realize that everything could have been arranged differently, better—that the time she'd spent there could have been wasted somehow. It had happened before.

Besides, she'd been busy. Sam hadn't been feeling well for a few days and she'd had to help him with shopping for food and furniture, with calling Con Ed and the phone company, and with finding warm clothes and blankets before winter started.

49

It was easier to arrange his life than it was to attend to her own. He needed the things she'd always had.

Last night she'd gone over to his place after work and cooked spaghetti for him, letting the sauce simmer for a long time so that his apartment would smell like food—like someone was living there. Afterwards they'd watched television until she became embarrassed about being there so late, and came home. Before she left she had given him her phone number, in case anything happened. It was something she'd been warned not to do by the people she worked with.

But there was something different about Sam. Most of her other clients either had lovers or family to care for them, or were more-or-less content to go on about their lives with minimal help from her. In Sam she thought she could sense something she understood: a need to turn and catch up the mismatched threads of the life behind him and weave them into something that he could understand, and that would keep. It was a kind of art, one she kept meaning to practice for herself, except that it was already hard enough to keep moments and hours and days from slipping away from her while at the same time trying to find a pattern in what had already passed.

For Sam it was even more desperate, more tied to time and the terror of realizing too late that it had been wasted. Anne assumed that she, at least, had plenty of time left, that at some point things would slow down to a tempo she could manage. Sam, even with his flickering bouts of hope for a cure, didn't have the luxury of making an assumption like that.

By degrees and successive sips of wine, Anne started to feel elation rising up from just below her ribs and, at the same time, from roughly the same place, the familiar faint fluttering of anxiety. She felt that something was beginning, something terrifying but definitely good because it was different. The sensation was like the one she had on an airplane that was moving up a runway at a speed that seemed impossible for something of that weight, shuddering, its nose lifting gradually *upward toward the thin air behind the clouds and a place she'd never gone before.*

She could help him. What he needed was a witness, a piece of film or paper onto which he could leave the images, and she could be that for him. She recognized what she was feeling now as a kind of love, but pure because it had nothing to do with their bodies.

The pieces of her own life fluttered behind her like ribbons to be wrapped around a Maypole.

Realization and Admission

There is an incomplete entry in my journal on November 4th:

It's possible that Grandma will die this week.

I'm becoming too involved with one of my clients, David E., and obsessed with somehow keeping him alive until they find a cure for AIDS.

Life is much more strange and complicated than

The entry ends there.

The First Night

One thing I do remember fairly clearly is how it was that I came to spend the night with David for the first time. He had moved into the apartment quite recently; it seems that he, his accident-in-the-process-of-happening veteran friend Dennis, and I were having a little housewarming party—just some beer, and maybe a little dinner. I guess that it must have gotten late. Dennis either had nowhere to go, or just lived too far away to want to travel home, and David offered to let him stay there. I'm certain that neither David nor I would have been bold enough to suggest that I stay the night too; it would have been Dennis (who was at least astute enough to see that neither David nor I would object if given the excuse) who convinced me.

Dennis ended up sleeping on the floor, and David and I were in the bed, both fully dressed. It never occurred to me that I should be apprehensive about spending the night with two heroin addicts (and ex-cons to boot), neither of whom I'd known more than a month or two, in a little studio apartment on the Lower East Side, with no one else knowing where I was. I just knew, somehow, that I had nothing to fear from David. I'm not sure if I touched him that night, but I would think that at some point I would have put my hand gently, surreptitiously, on his arm as he slept.

When David and I woke up the next morning, it was as if we were two people who'd gotten drunk the night before and ended up cheating on our spouses together. We were awkward with each other, nervous. I think David asked Dennis not to say anything about it to anyone. We both knew how much trouble I could get into if anyone found out—a trouble that could have gone beyond merely getting fired—and I think we both knew that it would happen again, and not for the sake of convenience. I knew, anyway.

Intersection

My grandmother, who had been in the hospital for a long time after breaking her leg because the doctors had found tumors all along her femur when they set it, was back home by early November. Every so often I'd take a day or two off from work and take the bus or train up to West Hartford to see her. She lay in her bedroom on a hospital bed much like the one David would eventually get to replace the futon mattress on the floor, while my grandfather sat confusedly in a chair beside her and occasionally told stories about their life together.

One weekend I drove up with my mother, and took the puppy, Sammy, along. I still don't know what made me think that it would be all right to let him out into the back yard late one morning; I guess we'd always done it with my grandparents' dog, and nothing had ever happened. In any case, I couldn't have been thinking very clearly.

Just as I realized that Sammy had disappeared, my grandmother—delirious from pain and painkillers—became very agitated.

"The black one...where's the black one?" she was saying. A few minutes later an officer of some sort came to the door to tell me that Sammy had been hit by a car, and was dead. He showed me Sammy's tiny purple collar, now bloodied.

I was hysterical. I must have gone to my grandmother for comfort, because I remember that I was next to her bed, sobbing, when David called a few minutes later. "Oh no," I remember him saying. "Oh no." I can still hear his voice saying it. He sounded genuinely upset. It still amazes me that he called at that moment.

That night I went home to my place in Hoboken. It was cold, and David, as usual, had a fever, but he made the hour-long trip from his apartment to mine in Hoboken because he knew that I needed him, because I had let "our" puppy get run over. He brought me a bouquet of flowers. I remember watching his face in the candlelight in the otherwise dark apartment.

My grandmother would die a month later, and David would die in April. I think of that moment, when I was at my grandmother's side and, at the same time, on the phone with David, Sammy having just been killed, as the intersection of death for that year, the eye in a storm of loss.

Watching Him Sleep

David's apartment building was on Suffolk Street, just off of Houston, up the block from a lesbian bar whose name at the time was Meow Mix. There was a tire-repair shop on the basement level of the building. It was run by a man named George, who would later prove his kindness by helping me with David in his last days.

David's apartment was one of three on the first floor. In the apartment next door lived a man who dressed in white robes that looked as if they'd been made from flannel sheets. We never spoke to him. It was rumored that his lover had died and that he had either somehow mummified him or simply left the body on his bed. He certainly looked capable of anything, and it was true that there was an odor of death around his apartment. (It was only recently that, while intentionally passing by the apartment building again, I ran into Mel—the man who had shown us the apartment in 1989—and he assured me that the story about the mummified body was, in fact, true).

But the smell could also have been caused by dead rats. There were cracks in the place where the floor met the walls, and at night we could see and hear the live ones trying to push their way into the apartment with their noses. I remember this with no sense of horror or disgust whatsoever; I seem to have simply taken it for granted, although I must have been aware that the rats' presence could be a real danger to someone with a compromised immune system.

But David was terrified of them. At night he would sometimes sit for hours on the edge of the bed, holding a large stick that he kept beside him there, cursing the rats, and cursing the man in the white robes, who, it was also rumored, kept them as companions along with his corpse. As far as I know, none of the rats ever actually made it into David's apartment.

Behind the building was another building from which a photographer's strobe light would flash at night. David used to wake up in a panic sometimes, thinking that they were lights from a police car.

As in many cheap downtown tenement apartments then, the bathtub was in the kitchen. I usually took my bath in the morning while David went to his methadone clinic; otherwise I'd do it while he was in bed. We'd bought one of those portable Japanese screens for privacy, as if we knew early on that I'd end up spending almost every night there.

There's an entry in my journal dated January 3rd, 1990, in which I describe sleeping with David. In the journal, I was still cautious enough to call him "Simon", but the fact that I wrote about it at all shows that the importance of wanting to remember as much as possible of my relationship with him was beginning to overshadow my fear of being found out:

Simon stops breathing every few minutes when he's asleep. He says that it has something to do with an irregularity in his heart, but every time it happens it seems to last a few more seconds than it should, so that I lay there next to him wide-awake wondering whether he'll breathe again, willing him to breathe again and completely conscious of my willing it. He's hard to sleep with. When he has a dream it's always a bad one, and he talks and twitches and gestures with his hands, often indicating so clearly what's happening in the dream that the whole thing seems staged.

Two or three weeks ago I woke up several times because he was sobbing, tearless, in his sleep. Then his left hand would lift from his chest and he would write through the air, line after line, and after a long time his hand would drop back down and he'd be still again, breathing and not breathing and breathing again. I described it to him, laughing so that he wouldn't be embarrassed about my watching him dream, and he told me that when his men were killed in Vietnam he took on the responsibility of writing to their families. It is so simple an explanation that I can barely believe it.

Later he started using his right hand to dial a telephone in his sleep. For this he had no explanation. Writing this now I realize that there must be something significant in the way that he was trying in different ways to communicate in his sleep, but I only come up with vague amateur theories that he'd politely consider but privately discard.

(Just now he woke and said, "You'd better get to sleep soon or you'll have trouble getting up in the morning." I asked him if the light was bothering him and he said, "No. I was just thinking of you." I believed him. A few seconds later, asleep again, he said, "Hell.")

An hour ago I took a Xanax and got into bed and tried to sleep. Simon had been sleeping while I watched an episode of China Beach, *one of a number of shows about Vietnam that have been on in the past year or two. The show was about romances starting or failing between the characters. In bed I started by lying on my side, facing Simon's back, and putting my hand lightly on his arm as I usually do. After a few minutes he turned over on his back and started to twitch and move his legs as if he might be running, whispering, "Hurry." He frowned and moved and opened his eyes a few times, and I remembered that when I asked him if I should wake him if I thought he was in "Vietnam" he said yes.*

So I said, "Simon."

He said, "Hm?"

I said, "Were you having a bad dream?"

"Yeah" (still mostly asleep).

He apologized, as he often does for no reason at all, and went back to sleep.

I got up to write this, have a beer and some cigarettes and another Xanax, and watch Simon sleep some more. Now I should try to sleep again so that I won't have too much trouble waking up in the morning.

Simon's talking again but I can't understand what he's saying.

I also wrote:

Since September I've spent fifteen or twenty hours watching Simon sleep. He sleeps more and more and I think I'm sleeping less, watching and listening and thinking and waiting to tell him what I've seen, heard, and thought. He shouldn't have to miss anything. I'm inadequate as a reporter, paying too much attention to details and often missing the scene as a whole, but I'm all he's got. Then again, he's seen more in 42 years than I probably ever will...I shouldn't be here anyway, but I am, and I will be until his breathing stops for good.

I rarely went home any more, but when I did—at least in the first couple of months—my life was in many ways the same as it had been before. I stayed out late, drank a lot with my friends at the local bars, and occasionally slept, platonically and in the spirit of camaraderie, with my ex-roommate Joe, a photographer who watched the slow progress of my shattering as the weeks and months passed, and soothed me with Calvados, music, good food made with ingredients he'd bought at Balducci's, and sensible conversation.

But it was never more than a night or two before I took the PATH train back into New York and rode the subway or the bus back down to Suffolk Street. I'd come in late at night, no doubt more often than not drunk, passing by the local junkies crouching between parked cars in the darkness to shoot up, and find David sitting up on the futon, or, later, in his wheelchair, in the gray-blue light of the television. Always quiet, always polite, he'd welcome me, and then I'd go into the bathroom, change into the flannel nightgown I left there, brush my teeth, and get into bed, and David would finally lie down. Gradually, I began to think of that place as my home. I felt safe there.

Holidays

I remember very little about which holidays David and I spent together, and how, if at all, we commemorated them. I can't imagine that I would have left him alone for any of them.

I found an entry from 16 October 1989 that mentions his birthday. Part of it got wet at some point and the ink ran, so part of it is illegible, but what I can put together of it says:

In six days it'll be David's birthday...short year ago that (I took him out) for lunch and he told me...about his life. (We were supposed to) go see (the building's owner) about his apartment, but it was pouring rain and (we didn't think he should) stay out in it so I bought him an umbrella and he walked me to the PATH station. I kissed him on the cheek and wished him happy birthday and he looked surprised, as I guess he should have been. Then I went home and he went back up to the Marion Hotel.

Autumn's got me thinking about him, too. And the fact that I actually did get TB from him. It's stupid, but I almost like the idea that I caught something from him. Any bond...

I don't know about Halloween. Even if he was in the apartment by then, Suffolk Street didn't strike me as a particularly likely place to get a lot of trick-or-treaters—at least not the kind who simply wanted candy.

On Thanksgiving I went into the city to pick him up, and brought him back to Hoboken to have dinner with my friend Joe and some friends. I know that I would have wanted him to have a good meal that day, and not be alone.

I have a shadow of a memory of going out with David to buy a Christmas tree one cold, overcast afternoon in December. We'd been sitting in the apartment, spending a weekend day in the usual way, when I decided that we had to get a tree for the apartment, and that we had to get it right away. David, always game for anything that would give him a chance to regain his bearings in a world in which simple little pleasures like holiday traditions were permitted and possible, followed me out the door and over to Essex, where we picked out the tree, and then helped me carry it back home. It would have had to have been a fairly small one, but I would have insisted that it be real so that the apartment would smell like Christmas. I seem to remember that David was too tired by the time we got home to help me decorate it with the cheap ornaments and lights that I'd bought in the discount stores on Delancey Street, and instead sat on the bed watching me do it with that happy, bemused little expression on his face as I hung ornaments and no doubt chattered on about Christmas. It was important to me that he at least have a tree for Christmas.

I was obligated to spend Christmas Day with my family in Connecticut, as I did every year, but David and I did spend Christmas Eve together. We'd spent the day on Suffolk Street, doing whatever it was that kept us happy and occupied back then. In the evening we went to my mother's apartment in Peter Cooper Village for dinner. David was nervous; we all were. He wanted to make a good impression. It had been, I think, a long time since he'd made a good impression on anyone other than me.

When we arrived, my mother was watching a show about tuberculosis on T.V. For a few minutes, we all just watched. No one knew what to say, or had the sense to turn it off. Other than that, the evening went fairly well. My mother gave David a green button-down shirt as a Christmas gift. (Years later,

63

my mother told me that she'd worried about eating from the plates and using the utensils that David had used afterwards. I was shocked to hear it, even thought that kind of thinking wasn't at all unusual at that time. Still, I was, and will always be grateful that she invited him to dinner that night.)

On New Year's Eve I know that I was with him. I remember the apartment being dim and vaguely festive, still scented with the pine-smell of the tree, lit either with candles or Christmas lights, or both. Late that night I sat on the bed and tried to call one of my favorite clients, a very young gay man named Jon, who was blessed with the most loving, supportive family I'd encountered in my time working with people with AIDS. His father answered, and told me that Jon was either sleeping or in the hospital–I don't remember which. Weeks later, I learned that Jon had actually died several weeks earlier. His father didn't want to upset me on New Year's Eve. The family had come to think of me as a friend, as Jon had.

Easter that year fell six days before David's death. I don't even know if we were aware of it; if not, that's probably for the best.

Details

I don't know if I can describe David in a way that would make anyone who didn't know him as I did understand why I was drawn to him, and why it was so easy for me to see past the violent, desperate life he had lived and the even more desperate circumstances that he had, at the end of his life, found himself in, and to love what I saw, and find peace in its presence. Then again, who can ever pinpoint what it is that makes her love a particular person—a person who, to others, might seem unremarkable, or even unworthy of love? I can only toss out some of the details that, to this day, make me smile when I remember them.

He was forty-two-and-half to the day on the day he died—fourteen years older than me. At the time, I thought of him as rather old. Of course, now that I'm over fifty myself, I've changed my thinking on that.

He was handsome, or at least I thought so. Even on the last day of his life, emaciated, dehydrated, and nearly drained of life, his face was beautiful. His eyes were huge (made even larger by the loss of weight, of course), and almost black. He had a way of looking into my eyes and holding my gaze, like a snake-charmer, but gentle, until he had made sure that I'd understood him. There was a white streak running through his black hair, which he had a tendency to brush straight back out of his face, although I always preferred it when it hung loose and curly. He had big hands, and a high forehead and cheekbones, and the skin on his body was almost hairless, and wonderfully smooth.

He could relate a story like no one I'd ever met, tossing in occasionally off-color (although he often apologized for that) similes and unexpected expressions, clearly enjoying immensely his own ability to weave the tale. No doubt the talent had served him well in many ways over the years. I've often thought that he should have been a writer, if he'd had the opportunity and someone to encourage him.

I remember him coming home one afternoon, shortly after I started spending nights at his apartment, with some things he'd bought on Delancey or Fourteenth Street—just some combs and razors, toothpaste and toothbrush, socks, underwear. He went through his bags, showing me everything. What would have seemed like the dullest of all possible shopping trips to most people clearly exhilarated him; it was obvious that having the leisure and the money (neither of which had to be spent immediately and without deliberation on drugs now that he was sticking to the methadone program) to buy a few simple things like any other man, made him very happy. I loved seeing him happy; in spite of everything that had happened and was going to happen, he could enjoy things more easily and fully than almost anyone I knew.

He hated Bob Vila, the *This Old House* guy. Despised him. He said that he used to work for him as a carpenter. I don't remember ever hearing him say that he hated anyone else, including the people who had abused him as a child, but he really had it in for Bob Vila. I wish I remembered what it was that Bob had done to be in such a unique position in David's mind.

He loved fried shrimp, and the only time I ever made it, as far as I remember, was for him, on a night when it was the only thing he could think of that he'd have an appetite for. He loved Katz's Deli on Houston Street (he introduced me to that, too), and, for reasons incomprehensible to me, Dinty Moore beef stew.

He apologized a lot, and he never forgot to say "please" or "thank you," even in his last days. It's rare, if ever, that I refer to anyone as a "gentleman", but he was a gentleman with me. Always.

On his right arm he had an old tattoo—just the word "*Diablo,*" in black. It looked as if it had been drawn with a Sharpie pen onto his right arm; I think he said that he'd gotten it in prison when he was much younger. Because he'd lost so much weight it had become a little distorted-looking. I teased him one day a little as we sat on his bed about the fact that it was a terrible tattoo, and that he didn't seem devilish in the least, and I remember the amused and slightly confused expression on his face as he smoked a cigarette (we both smoked Marlboros) and listened to my theories (when I imagine the scene it seems to me that I was being a little flirtatious, romping around him on the bed like an affectionate puppy while he watched me, indulgent and slightly paternal). I gather that mine was the minority opinion on that subject, and not one that he was used to hearing.

Sometimes, when he was sitting on the futon, watching T.V., he looked like a kid watching cartoons on a Saturday morning, transfixed and giggling. He laughed and smiled easily and often; his laugh was quiet and a little mischievous, but there was, when I think about it now, always a little sadness in his eyes, a pleading look that I know wasn't feigned, even when he was laughing.

He never asked me for anything, or took anything from me, as an addict might be expected to do. On the contrary, he would often, for example, give me

67

money when I was broke (which was fairly often). When, selfishly, I asked him for a sip of his precious methadone (of which he really needed every drop) so that I could sleep, he gave it to me without question. On the other hand, he never tried to get me to take any drugs.

I saw him high, I believe, two times. Once he'd obviously done heroin or too much methadone, and was nodding over dinner at a restaurant on Avenue A (where, at least, it wasn't an unusual sight). The other time his behavior was so manic, so unlike him, so uncharacteristic of any drugs I could imagine him taking (I know that narcotics were his "drug of choice" because he had a tendency toward anxiety and anything else would have been likely to make that worse), that I've always wondered if what I was seeing might actually have been the beginnings of dementia, or an unusual reaction to something he'd ordinarily be used to.

I also wondered for a long time how and why a man with such a long history of heavy heroin use, and with what few people would see as much of any reason to live at that point, David otherwise never strayed from his methadone program during the time I knew him, at least as far as I could tell. In his neighborhood, it would have been much easier to walk no more than half a block from the building, get a bag of heroin, and really get high (and even, with an apartment of his own, do it in a warm, safe place for a change), than it was to get up early every morning, even in the cold, to take two buses to the methadone clinic— when the prescribed dose of methadone would not have even gotten him high, but only kept him from getting sick. That was, in my experience, unusual, but at the time, for some reason, I didn't give it much thought (there was, admittedly, a lot to which I didn't give much thought). Now, however, I believe that he was just trying to conduct the last few months of his life with as much dignity as possible.

Once, when he was at my apartment in Hoboken, I listened to the messages on my answering machine in his presence. I was mortified when he heard a message from my mother, in which she warned me to "be careful with him"—meaning that I should take care not to catch whatever it was he had. If it angered him, or upset him, he never let on. When he met her some time after that, he was perfectly polite.

On the cold afternoon on which, impulsively or after a period of deliberation, he suddenly reached his hand over to touch my cheek and turn my face toward his—an invitation to a kiss—and I simply looked at him, confused and without even the grace to explain, there was no reproachful, angry, or bitter reaction. He only smiled a regretful little smile and looked down, his look clearly saying, "I understand. I'm sorry. I'll never do that again." And he didn't. I wish he had.

When he could do something for himself, he did. He never expected me to wait on him, although I would always be glad to. Aside from simply mentioning it when something in particular was hurting him or making him feel more sick than usual, he never (although he had every right to) whined or complained about how he felt, and he never portrayed himself as a "victim" of AIDS. Maybe he'd simply been convinced, like so many people around him, that he'd brought it on himself, and that he deserved to die like that.

O.I.'S

"AIDS" is a meaningless acronym, especially for someone who has never had first-hand experience with it; it gives no indication of what the disease is capable of doing to a person's body when there's nothing to stop it or effectively slow it down.

The "letter of introduction" that allowed people with AIDS access to social services back then was called the "M11-Q." In about three pages, it distilled a client's life down to what were considered the essentials—housing status (either an address or another coy term—"undomiciled"), sources of income or benefits already in place, brief psychological profile (basically, whether the client knew where and who he was, or if he had been diagnosed with a mental illness or addiction), prescribed medications, and the often-daunting list of known, AIDS-defining opportunistic infections.

David fell more-or-less in the mid-range in terms of the number of O.I.'s listed on his M11-Q on the day I met him; there were probably four or five listed (no doubt he picked up more in the following months).

I'm certain that he had tuberculosis—I came down with it shortly after he died—and toxoplasmosis. He had wasting syndrome, although I never realized how much weight he'd already lost until, years later, his sister told me that she'd cried over how thin he'd become when I sent her a picture of him. (He'd weighed, she estimated, at least a hundred pounds more the last time she'd seen him, almost ten years earlier.) The skin hung from his once-muscular arms in useless folds. No doubt he'd already had PCP pneumonia at least once.

He may have also had lymphoma. For a long time he had an enormous lump on one side of his neck, over his lymph node, and then it broke open and we had to clean and bandage it every day. It took a long time to heal; in fact, I don't know that it ever did completely. I cleaned it for him, sometimes wearing a pair of latex gloves from the box supplied by the visiting nurse, and sometimes—when I simply didn't have it in me to humiliate him any more—not. (I knew enough about HIV to know that it wouldn't get through unbroken skin, or the mythical "microscopic abrasions" that uninfected people fretted about.)

One thing he *didn't* have was Kaposi's Sarcoma, which seemed to vindictively plague only the gay men most obsessed with their looks, the handsome young men who had come to New York to escape their mundane or dangerous lives at home and make their fortunes as models or actors, now reduced to trying to camouflage their enormous black-purple lesions with thick layers of makeup.

Later, in his last few months, the skin all over David's body (which, when I first met him, was smooth, nearly hairless, and hard to resist touching) was dry and flaky and cracked, and I think that he also had peripheral neuropathy, which would have made his hands both painful and numb. AZT had made his fingernails black.

And yet, on the day I met him, he was still considered relatively healthy. That's how bad things were back then.

It seems important that I describe here what it's like to have active tuberculosis, which was just a minute piece of what David, and many of my other clients, had to deal with.

I remember being in the shower, perhaps a month or two after David died, and feeling lumps under my

71

arms; I didn't think about it much, because I was still thinking about David pretty much all of the time and not paying attention to much else. I knew that something was wrong, but I really didn't care. A few months after that, I began to sweat at night to the point where whatever I was sleeping in would become soaking wet. I was exhausted, but sleeping became all-but-impossible because of the excruciating–really excruciating–pain all up and down my back, and because I shivered uncontrollably, just as David had when I tried to warm him at night. I don't remember coughing, but I lost fifteen or twenty pounds in probably less than a month.

When I finally went to see my doctor, he gave me a TB test–just a little four-pronged jab in the arm (just one, in my case). Late that night, or maybe the night after, the spot where he'd jabbed me had swollen up into a painful, itching lump the size of a walnut. Mystery solved.

I started a regimen of three drugs. One of them was Rifampin, which was the drug that sucked away almost all of methadone's efficacy and therefore forced anyone on a program who also had the disease into a difficult choice between withdrawal and a worsening of the illness with the threat of quarantine, and to which I had such a severe reaction that I spent two separate nights in the emergency room, nauseated, dizzy, and burning up from the inside out. I remember being in the ER waiting room the second time it happened, feeling that I might die, and having a nurse wordlessly toss a mask at me from across the room, and leave again as the other people in the waiting room turned to stare at me. That kind of thing happened a lot; I'd never felt like a pariah before, never quite understood (although I suppose I thought I did) how thoroughly my clients were made to feel that they were monsters, unfit to be around the well, unwelcome, and deserving to be so. And I was a straight white girl, with a job and no drug habit to speak of, and I didn't even have AIDS.

And yet, if I'd had to go through it all again just to have one of those days with David back, I'd have done it, without question. I still would. I wouldn't even have to choose the day–any one of them would do.

Love, and the Long Road Down

The second-to-last entry I made in my journal about my life with David while he was still alive was on New Year's Day, 1990. It reads:

On December 5 Grandma died at home.

Coming back from the funeral in Connecticut, I went directly to Suffolk Street. It was a very cold night. David surprised me by standing up (it seems that that may have been the first time I noticed that it was hard for him to get up from the bed) and putting his arms around me when I came in—something he'd never done before then. I got the impression that it was something he'd been rehearsing in his head all day—not that it was insincere, but only something that he wasn't used to doing any more. I certainly needed it, at any rate; as usual, he'd known that instinctively.

If I had to name one thing that made me love David more than anything else, it would be that he did things like that. Things that might seem relatively ordinary in a man who had lived under ordinary circumstances—a consoling hug; a long trip in the cold to bring a gift of flowers; a shoulder- or foot-massage; an easy willingness to give me whatever I asked for, or what I needed but didn't ask for; a gentle, protective touch; kind and thoughtful advice when something was upsetting me—were not so easily expected from a man who had lived under labels like "delinquent", "junkie", "convict", and "homeless man" for much of his life. And I still don't understand how a man from whom love had been withheld pretty much from the day he was born was able to give it so gracefully, and without asking

74

for anything in return. Somehow, it seemed to come naturally for him.

The very last page that I wrote on in the journal, on January 26th, contains no real entries, only David's biological mother's telephone number scrawled at the top with "David's Evil Mom" beneath it, and a list of things to remember for later. The latter, it seems, suggests that I somehow knew that I wouldn't be writing again for a long time, that from there on out I'd be taking the last steps on the long road down, that what I'd find at the bottom would require all my energy, leaving nothing to spare at the end of any given day.

One of the items on the list reads:

--not going out anywhere any more

I'm pretty sure that "not going out anywhere" referred to my old life at home, and not to my life with David. Going out to the bars in Hoboken no longer held any appeal for me whatsoever. On the rare evenings I spent at home, I'd pass the time smoking, drinking wine, and listening to music until David called or I simply went back to Suffolk Street on my own, like a bird who had made her nest elsewhere.

David and I did go out together, when he was well enough. On weekend mornings we'd go to Benny Burrito's on Avenue A, or to a Dominican place a few blocks away from the apartment, for a late breakfast. Sometimes we had dinner in the East Village, and sometimes we'd just walk for hours. He loved the city, and he loved to walk. We'd do the kinds of things that I was used to doing already, conducting ourselves as if the lives we'd lived before meeting each other had not been so different, finding a common ground that became more and more familiar. We were, in many ways, not all that different;

it was only through freakishly good luck, or the attentions of some benevolent angel, that I was not in the position that he was in. I must have told him that. I hope I did.

We went to two movies together—*Drugstore Cowboy*, and *Born on the Fourth of July*. There's a notation in my journal about something happening after *Born on the Fourth of July*, but I don't remember what it was. Something in the film must have set David off, or just depressed him. I wish I remembered.

It was more fun to see *Drugstore Cowboy* with David. He pointed out several inaccuracies, such as a technical error regarding the injection of Dilaudid (you don't cook it, apparently), about which, in spite of some hands-on experience in the field, I would have otherwise been in the dark.   In retrospect, I can't imagine what I was thinking, taking a man who was trying to kick a thirty-year heroin habit to a film in which drug use is so lovingly and graphically portrayed.   What kept David from bolting from the Angelika Theatre out onto Houston to score the nearest bag of heroin he could find is beyond me.

It seems to me now that it was after one of those two movies that I at least briefly acknowledged consciously to myself for the first time that I was falling in love with David.   I have a dreamlike memory of getting out of a taxi with him on Houston Street near the apartment, fairly late at night.   I remember that I was wearing the black wool Afghan hat that I always wore over my pixie-cut hair, and I would have been wearing dangly earrings, dark eye shadow, deep wine-colored lipstick, and in all likelihood my straight black wool coat and black leggings—the uniform of the late-80's New York social worker/Bohemian wannabe. No doubt I'd had a few glasses of wine or something somewhere

(David actually drank very little, but I had a healthy appetite for alcohol).   And I remember suddenly being very happy at the thought that I was with David, and that we'd be spending another night together. He seemed happy, too; I remember that we were both laughing, almost giddy, as we stepped out of the taxi into the cold night, brightly lit with streetlights and neon from the stores on Houston.

There's another memory I have—just a flash, really—of a realization that there was nowhere I wanted to be but at David's. I have no idea when it happened, but it was one of those beautiful late afternoons in Manhattan, and I'd just finished visiting one of my other clients in Stuyvesant Town on Fourteenth Street. The workday was over and I had my Walkman on, as usual; it was playing T. Rex's *Electric Warrior* as I walked down Avenue A or B toward the Suffolk Street apartment, and, again, I was happy.

The list also includes this:

--being afraid to look at anything beautiful

I don't know whether it was David or me who was afraid to look at anything beautiful, but I suspect that it was me. I'd known for a long time that the things I tended to think of as the most beautiful were the kinds of things that couldn't last, and by then that knowledge must have been unbearable.

Fights

We fought sometimes. Or, I should say, I fought with him; he never raised his voice to me, or lost his temper. I was not so forbearing.

In a wirebound notebook, I made another, final list less than a week after David died of the things I wanted to remember about him. One of the entries on the list is a reminder of something I lost my temper about, probably more than once:

--missed app'ts., etc.—demand to know whether he's going to let himself die

It was a strange and willfully naive way to phrase it—"let himself die." The fierce, blind tenacity of my outrageous belief that we had any control over things beyond a temporary stay of execution must have outlived his. I was furious when I found out that he'd been missing his appointments at the V.A. Hospital's Infectious Disease clinic (not the methadone clinic appointments, ever). But it was to be expected, if you think about it realistically. As I mentioned earlier, one of the TB drugs—Rifampin—had the effect of rendering methadone nearly useless, causing withdrawal. The effects of AZT could be as bad as those of some of the infections themselves. Besides, as I just said, my hope for a miracle must have long outlasted his; he knew the accelerating process of the failure of his body more intimately than I ever could. Maybe he'd just stopped seeing the point, and was instead seeing through to the reality that I kept denying—that, back then, there was no treatment that would save him. AIDS was not a "manageable illness."

There were other things. I gave him a ring that I used to wear, a silver twist of two dolphins that I'd bought for a few dollars on vacation somewhere, because he liked it, and because I secretly liked the idea of his wearing my ring. He came home from the methadone clinic without it one day. Another client had admired it so much, he said, that he had to give it to her. I suspect that he actually traded it for some extra methadone from someone (as far as I know, there weren't many female clients in the V.A. methadone clinic). Everyone "doubled up" whenever possible. To be too outraged by this would be hypocritical—sometimes I took a sip too. It relieved me of anxiety for a while, and helped me sleep.

I think that my fury over the missing ring took David by surprise. Of course it did. I'd been too much of a coward to give him any indication of what his wearing the ring meant to me, or of my visions of what kind of relationship we would have had under different circumstances (it's telling, I think, that he very wrongly assumed that telling me that he'd given the ring to a woman would be upset me less than telling me what I believe to be the actual truth—that he used it to get extra methadone). He must have thought that my confused lack of a response the one time he tried to kiss me had told him all he needed to know, and he was enough of a gentleman to let it go at that.

Of course, it was strange to come straight to work from Suffolk Street in the morning and get to work on David's case, along with the cases of my twenty-nine or so other clients. Some of my co-workers were aware of what I was doing, and my friends among them warned me to be careful, as if it weren't already much too late, as if I could or would have changed anything at that point.

I'm sure that I was just as inept with David's paperwork as I was with everyone else's. I don't think

The Unanswered Prayer

If the progression of David's illness that winter was noticeable beyond, perhaps, more frequent fevers and his sleeping more and more, I must not have allowed myself to acknowledge it. I doggedly went about the business of doing everything I could think of to keep him going—scrubbing out the bathtub every day before he took his bath, washing eggs before I cooked them, keeping him warm by any means possible, still hounding him to keep his clinic appointments and take his meds and drink his Sustecal so that he wouldn't lose too much more weight, making sure he ate properly. He was probably sitting up more at night by then, watching for the rats, thinking thoughts that sometimes put that sweet, mysterious, lost little smile on his face.

One evening, probably some time in February, sitting on the edge of the futon, he started to chant in a high, broken voice, almost oblivious to my presence. When I asked him what he was doing, he told me that he was singing Chippewa prayers, "to take this thing from my body." By the following morning, his formerly unwavering optimism that he would somehow beat the virus seemed to have just disappeared. He must have felt overnight that his body had gone past the point of no return, and come to understand that the prayer, his last hope, would not change things. There's a notation in the journal I wrote just after he died about how he looked that morning over breakfast at our Dominican restaurant, the hood of his blue sweatshirt pulled up over his head, his eyes huge, sadder than I'd ever seen anyone's eyes look. He hardly spoke—something which, for a man as talkative as David had always

81

been, was alarming in itself. I seem to remember reaching across the table to take his hand and sitting there with him in silence, but perhaps that's only what I wished I'd done, in retrospect.

According to the journal, we spent most of the rest of that day in bed.

On a Monday morning, shortly after that, I woke up to find his mind gone. At first, I thought he was dead, but he was breathing, still warm, and his eyes were open. But he wasn't really there; he didn't seem to hear me begging him to wake up, or feel me touching him to try to get him to respond.

The Visiting Nurse Service sent someone over. I don't remember anything about her except that she was cold, and brusque, and obviously thought I was a fool for being there in the first place. She took David's temperature; it was 105 degrees. She told me that he'd be dying soon, that I'd just have to wait it out, that it wouldn't be long, that there was nothing to be done. And then she left.

I called in sick to work. All I remember of the rest of that day was the quiet, and the way the white winter light from the windows moved slowly across the floor as the time went by and I waited for David to die. I think I was frightened of him as much as I was frightened for him, for some reason, but I spent most of the day sitting on the floor next to the bed, talking to him, cooling his forehead with damp cloths, stroking his hair. It was, I realized a long time later, a kind of rehearsal for what would come in April. As it turned out, I played my part better the first time around.

He didn't die. At some point late in the afternoon, miraculously, he came back to consciousness, and I took him to the hospital, where he could at least, I thought, be safe and relatively comfortable. At least I hoped so.

My hopes were in vain; they punctured his lung right off the bat. They must have been trying to find out if he had PCP, or maybe they were checking his lungs for something having to do with the TB. They probably did a spinal tap, too; I don't remember if David had had one before then, but he was terrified of them. He was also afraid of needles and I.V.'s, at least when they were administered by someone other than him, because most of the veins in his arms had collapsed over the years. Sometimes a doctor or nurse would let him find a good vein and get the needle in himself. Sometimes they would just stick him in the groin, where the veins were still good. That, he said, was incredibly painful.

I don't know what it was that made his mind shut down that morning. Toxoplasmosis can cause lesions on the brain—maybe that was it. In any case, he began his hospital stay on oxygen, and with a punctured lung in danger of collapsing altogether at any time. He looked so small and scared in his hospital bed, silently watching me yell at the doctors.

The doctors, for the most part, were young and arrogant interns who just didn't seem to understand why I would be so upset about the lung. With a few rare and wonderful exceptions, most doctors confronted with a junkie with AIDS were either of the "he-brought-it-on-himself" or the "he's-going-to-die-anyway" camp, or both. Both ways of thinking were, it could be argued, correct. But that wasn't the point. Thinking that way, and treating a person accordingly, were two very different things. I didn't give a damn what they thought. All I wanted was for David to be treated well, and as if a miracle were possible, if things were just done properly.

Hospital

David's lung didn't collapse. He was, however, in the hospital for about a month, possibly longer. My mother was living in the Peter Cooper Village apartment I'd lived in as a child, just down First Avenue from the V.A. Hospital and from Bellevue, where David would die in April. I started going over there after work to wait for the evening visiting hours to begin. On weekends I'd spend most of my time at the hospital, passing the time between visiting hours at the apartment.

Once he was able to start eating again, I'd usually bring David some dinner, or something else that I thought might make him happy. In the evenings I'd wheel him in his wheelchair into the waiting room, where it was unlikely that anyone who wasn't a patient would be waiting because it was rare that anyone visited the patients on that floor, but where the veterans with AIDS who were able to sit up gathered to watch television and share war stories from Vietnam (almost everyone, it seemed, was a Navy SEAL or a Green Beret; listening to them, one would think that there had been no regular soldiers whatsoever in Vietnam) or from the streets of New York. We all used to watch *Jeopardy* together.

Sometimes I'd just sit in David's room and watch him sleep; sometimes I did the things for him that the nurses wouldn't do, like rub lotion into his cracked and peeling skin, or wash his feet, which had become so swollen that he'd never be able to wear his boots again. The second in the series of poems I wrote about him years later was about a long Sunday afternoon when he didn't have the strength to leave his room:

84

How You Looked
(V.A. Hospital, Spring, 1990)

David, let me wash and cool
Your swollen feet while you're awake
So nothing can get worse, at least
For now, at least not here where we
Are so alone, the nurses masked,
Reluctant to come in the room.

I'd almost tell you how you looked
Asleep, all afternoon,
Your body on a boat
Losing course, slipping over fish, the sun
A yellow wine that whispered
In my head to let you drift.
I watched your face fall fully
Open, saw your sheets come loose
And drop apart, your body a mirage,
Your belly hollowed-out and vaporous,
Your penis arched and cool
Dozing there, flawless in the glare.

The sound is just the rush
Of water and a washcloth
In a bowl. Tell me if it feels too hot
Or cold. You'll feel my fingers
Run across your toes so thick
I'll never pass a towel through. Your skin
Is breaking up like desert floor,
No longer big enough to hold you in.

Although I stopped writing about David, or
anything else, in my journal after January of that year,
I did, years later, find something scribbled on a

tattered piece of notebook paper among David's things that I must have written on another day in the hospital, while David was sleeping:

MARCH

This only happens on certain afternoons when the sky is a certain way, blue hinting at silver and the kind of quiet that seems to be made up of thousands of leaves brushing together in wind, but muted, and the occasional sound of a far-off helicopter. It may even have some meaning, if I let myself think of things that way, but I'm afraid that if I start to look for good omens then I'll have to admit to the force of bad ones, too. The thumbnail moon that came up over Chelsea on the first night Simon was admitted, for example. He was too weak and spaced out from fever and four days of not eating to get up and see it (for all I know he was hallucinating little moons of his own, there behind his frightened poster-child eyes), and I was too exhausted to describe it to him. I thought it might mean that there was hope that he'd get well again, at least for a while, but I could see other things through the window—the stopped clock on the Con Ed tower, for instance—that could just as easily mean something else. So I said, "There's a new moon. It's pretty," and let it go at that. Simon didn't answer.

Anyway, the thing that happens on those particular afternoons (which are fairly frequent because we've been having a premature, hot spring) is that I'll look out the hospital window down over the streets and buildings around which I happened to spend my childhood, and I'll momentarily recall with amazing clarity of detail and feeling a dream I had when I was six or seven. At the time, I was learning to swim at the public bathhouse and pool near the river, at the end of Twenty-third Street. A corner of it is visible from Simon's window, and from the dayroom you can look almost right down over the building and into the now waterless pool. The dream wasn't all that long or involved or even exciting; I'm just surprised that it's stayed with me for over twenty years.

Somehow in the dream I'm dropped down onto or lifted up to a place which, had I known what the V.A. Hospital was at the time, would have been the center of its roof. Then, after looking for a few moments at the pool and streets and shorter buildings below me, and listening to the helicopters over the river and the slow swirl of hot wind around the roofs and spires, I simply drop down into the air and fly a little. I circle the building once or twice, high enough to be looking down at the gulls and a plane. Then I softly land again, and the dream, or what I remember of it, ends. Few things that I've done or dreamed since have felt so good, and it embarrasses me a little to admit that I still have a feeling that I've flown and could do it again.

So it's comforting sometimes to turn from Simon's bed to the bright window, to forget for a few minutes that Simon may sink further into this black hole of fever and infection and dementia and never come back.

I must have known by then that no omen, good or bad, was going to change things, but I was no more able to admit that to either of us than I was to admit to David that I was in love with him.

The Conversation

There was an entry in the blog that I wrote many years later that described what had seemed like a small, unrelated incident (but one that had upset me a great deal at the time, and had continued to haunt me) that had happened at some point after David's death, but that turned out to be the best way to describe what I was feeling in early spring of 1990, when David was discharged for the last time from the V.A. Hospital:

A few years ago, I was on a cruise ship, watching the water through my cabin window. We were well out to sea. I noticed a tiny bird flying alongside the ship, close to the water. As far as I could tell, he wasn't a seabird; he was one of the little birds who fly onto ships when they're in port, and end up sailing along to the next destination. He must have flown a little too far away from the ship while we were at sea, and I could tell that he was desperately trying to catch up with us, flapping his wings wildly to stay above the water. But we were moving too fast, and I knew that he'd never get back to the ship. I could feel his panic and exhaustion inside me as I watched, helpless to do anything to save him. Every so often he'd hit the water, or a wave would slap up at him, but for a long time he kept coming back up to fly a little more. It was, however, only a matter of time, and he must have known it. Finally he went down for good, and the ship sailed on without him.

I would not have been human if I didn't allow myself to believe, despite evidence to the contrary, that once David was released from the hospital everything would be the same as it had been before he went in. In another kind of world, and in a time other than the late 1980's, that would have been how things normally went: most people went into the hospital, were treated, recovered, and went home. No one was sent home until he could reasonably be expected to live, or had made a deliberate decision to go home to die.

It was, at least, an early spring; David wouldn't have to be cold any more. If we'd made mistakes in the past, I'd make sure that we didn't make them again—I would clean more thoroughly, cook better food, make sure that David never missed a dose of anything.

To be honest, I don't remember exactly what I was thinking the day he was discharged. But, at least in his first few days at home, what else could I have thought? Springtime was not a time to die.

In spite of everything that I so desperately wanted to believe, however, the evidence that things would not, in fact, be the same as they'd been before David went into the hospital was difficult to ignore. When he came home, he had a wheelchair, a cane, a walker, boxes of gauze bandages, bottles of purified water, two home health attendants, and a brand-new hospital bed. As his caseworker, I would have arranged for all of it, as I would have for any of my clients.

He didn't want to sleep in the new bed; he still usually slept on the futon mattress on the floor, with me.

We never went out together again, and David was no longer able to make his morning run to the methadone clinic (he was given the little bottles to drink at home when the hospital discharged him).

I don't remember the first time we spoke about what would happen when he died, about how he wanted it to happen at home, about what he wanted me to do with his body. I don't remember who brought it up first, but I hope it wasn't me.

89

At work, one of the first things we learned in our trainings was that when a client started to speak about the eventuality of his or her own death, the worst thing that we could do would be to try to change the subject, pretend that it wouldn't happen, say inane, cheery things. We were to follow the client's lead, and simply listen well enough to know how to make him or her feel that it was all right to talk about it.

The conversations we had about it are vague memories, but I have a picture in my mind of David standing near the kitchen (although, in retrospect, he wouldn't have been able to stand on his own, or carry on much of a conversation, after he came home from the hospital, so perhaps he was sitting in his wheelchair), and me sitting on the bed, talking about it. I just can't remember the words. But it seems that we spoke almost casually about it; my impression now is that he did that for my benefit more than his own.

I think I remember talking about a cherry tree. I must have also mentioned that much of the area around my mother's house on Long Island is sacred ground, burial ground, for the local Shinnecock Indians. That would have appealed to him; his Native American identity always meant a great deal to him.

However it was decided when he was alive, I had a plan by the time he died. I wrote about it—coincidentally, I think—on April 30th, the day his body was cremated:

When I get his ashes I'm going to plant a tree in Hampton Bays and scatter them around its roots and when the tree bears fruit I'll eat it, and he'll finally be inside me.

I asked him once what I should do with my life—whether I said it or not, he would have known perfectly well that I meant, "What will I do when you're gone?" He told me that I should get married, have a child. I'm almost certain that I told him then that all I wanted was his child. We may have even talked about how we might be able to make that happen without my getting infected. It was all just fantasy, of course, just as our conversations about leaving the city and living in the country, or by the beach, was fantasy. But it was a fantasy that I desperately needed to believe in then, and he allowed me to do it.

The Unforgivable

One of the most difficult, if not the most difficult, entries to read among any of the records I kept of my time with David was written about two weeks after he died, and it was one of the things that kept me awake, sobbing with guilt, night after night, all those years later.

The journal entry, dated May 5th, 1990--about two weeks after David's death—is an account something that happened within the few weeks before he died:

I took a day and went home and thought about him until I wasn't angry at him any more. The night before, I'd called him and he'd asked me to come down and see him. When I got there, thinking that I was going to spend the night with him, he told me that he wanted to sleep alone, that he'd tried to call to tell me, but I'd already left. All the anger and frustration that I'd been trying to control while he was sick came out then, because he was rejecting me and that was the one thing I could never bear to have him do. It didn't matter to me then that he was in pain and terrified and aware that he was losing his mind and his life. He was my lover, and he didn't want me to sleep with him. I screamed and kicked things and called him selfish and thoughtless and weak. He put his head in his hands and said, "Oh, God," but I couldn't stop. I despised him because he could bear to spend one of his last nights without me. He tried to explain that he just wanted to be in bed alone and use all the pillows and try to get some sleep, but I wouldn't let myself believe him.

Later, when I stopped screaming and sat silent in his wheelchair, watching television, still furious, he started to slide toward me on the bed. I thought that he was going to touch me, take my hand, but I wasn't sure so I did nothing. He put his hand on the arm of the wheelchair; he was trying to get up. I said nothing and did nothing to help him. After a while I got up to leave. I must have said something before I left, but I don't remember what. In any case I didn't say goodbye, even though it occurred to me that he might die during the night as I was opening the door, which I slammed when I went out.

It makes me sick now that I treated him like that.

The day I went home to think I read the chapter on "Acceptance" in On Death and Dying.

I don't remember whether it was David or me who was the first to call and try to make things O.K. between us again. It certainly should have been me, because what I did was unforgivable, evil. I know for certain that David, true to form, never reproached me for what I'd done, and that when I finally went back he made me feel as at-home as ever.

Thinking about it, my only consolation is that there's a possibility that my bad behavior (that, and my somehow telling him that I'd want his child) had finally made him understand, without my having to say it outright, that I loved him.

Bath

Although, like a wounded lion whose strength had always been the key to his survival, he fought for a very long time against his weakness, David, my older man, my talkative, story-weaving, walk-loving former badass whose arms had once been as big as trees, became as dependent as a child in those last few weeks. I'd had to arrange for a nurse to come in during the day when I was at work, but otherwise I was always there. It never seemed like a chore or a hardship for me. There was nowhere else I wanted to be, and it was hard for me to trust David's care to anyone else.

When, shortly after David's death, I used to hold his shirt to my face to smell him in it, it smelled only of cigarette smoke, and of something slightly sweet, like maple syrup, and perhaps of something a little medicinal. I don't remember ever thinking that he smelled bad, even after he was too sick to bathe for weeks (toward the end, though, he thought that he did). But at some point I must have panicked at the thought that not bathing would somehow affect his health, and one morning I insisted that he have a bath in our tub in the kitchen. Maybe I also thought that it might help him feel a little better.

It was not something that he wanted to do; he was, at that point, too weak to do it without my help and, although he didn't say it, it was obvious that he was embarrassed about having me see him naked. I assumed that it was because he was so thin by then, and any muscle he'd had had wasted away, but I also think that it had been a long time since a woman had seen him undressed.

94

I still remember how he turned toward the wall as he took off his clothes, how his face looked when he sat down in the bath I'd run for him, how big his dark eyes were, how small he seemed. He looked like a frightened child, and he wouldn't, or couldn't, talk. I didn't want to hurt or embarrass him, but I forced him to do it because I was afraid for him. I wrote this poem about it, years later:

BATH

Shock of water when you dropped, at last,
Into your bath: you had not
Undressed in weeks, much less
In front of me. Discreet, my fingers
Which had for weeks in secret
Decoded death's maneuvers on your back's
Cracked skin, once sleek to touch
As glass, my fingers which had felt
For fever on your brow
And found it, which had tapped the tempo
Of the lonely thoughts we'd had
Together, the dreaming symphonies.

Squeezing water
Down from your neck, passing soap
In timid measures along inches
Of your flesh, I startled
Nests of outraged sparrows
From where they'd safely slept.

He'd go for days without being able to eat. I'd try to get him to drink water, or get a little Sustecal down when he could, but even that was hard for him. The only thing he was taking in on a regular basis was morphine, which had been prescribed for him in the hospital, and methadone. At one point I expressed

95

concern that he was possibly taking too much. He looked at me with that mischievous little kid's smile and said, "There's a method to my madness."

To this day, I'm still not sure exactly what he meant by that. Getting high certainly was no longer a priority for him (it hadn't been for a very long time). Because he complained so rarely, I think that I allowed myself to be unaware of how much pain he must have been in, even since before I met him. Sometimes I wonder if he was trying to hasten the end at that point. I was selfish enough at that point that it would have hurt me to think that he wouldn't want to prolong his life for my sake.

The Journey

David's veteran buddies where about the most loyal band of heroin addicts you'd ever want to meet. They'd usually run into each other in the morning in the V.A.'s methadone clinic. Afterwards, they would all go to the Malibu coffee shop on Twenty-Third Street and have breakfast and some coffee to help the methadone kick in. David loved doing that; he always talked about it when he came home. He was proud to have friends who seemed to really care about him.

Among the friends were Dennis, a loquacious, affable pile of trouble (and the man to whom I'll always be grateful for seeing to it that David and I slept together for the first time, considering that both of us were too shy to have ever managed it on our own), and Richie, who was also big, and Irish-looking, and very kind. There was Frank, who, although not the sharpest needle in the bag, was a goofy sweetheart who later gave me his parents' phone number on Long Island so that I could call them and let them know if he died. And there was Robin, who was quieter than the others, with long, dark hair. He was the one who wrote and delivered David's eulogy at the memorial service. Something about him frightened me a little. It wasn't that he seemed threatening, but he had a way of looking at people very intently, as if he was searching for any signs of hypocrisy, any weakness.

I suppose they're all dead by now. I hope not, but I think that they all had AIDS, and people didn't live 24 years (which, I've read, is now the life expectancy of a person infected with HIV these days) after a diagnosis back then. Back then, 24 months would have been considered a particularly magnanimous favor from God.

At some point in the few days before he died, David must have run out of the methadone he'd been allowed to take home from the hospital. He didn't seem to care, but my thinking was that he shouldn't have to go through withdrawal along with everything else, so I called the methadone clinic, and they agreed to give him more if I could get him over there. I guess they wanted to make sure that it was for him.

I remember the process of getting him out of the apartment, down the stairs, into a taxi, and upstairs to the clinic as a kind of parade. I don't remember exactly who was with us, but I know that it was several of his V.A. buddies, as well as one of his home attendants. George, from the tire shop, helped us get David and his wheelchair outside and into a cab.

Sitting in the back seat of the taxi with David, I pointed out the cherry blossoms and forsythia that had bloomed on some streets since he came home from the hospital. It was a warm spring day—perfect for an outing. David looked at what I showed him, and smiled a little, but he was too weak to say much of anything. His head was on my shoulder, and my arm was around him.

When we got to the V.A. clinic, all the junkies became soldiers again, standing and greeting David respectfully as I wheeled him through in his wheelchair, as if he were a returning hero. His counselor, too, greeted him kindly; by that time I understood David well enough to know that the reception was making him very happy, even if he had only the strength to smile and raise his hand a little in greeting.

David had to sign some sort of paper in order to get his methadone; it was almost impossible for him to do. The counselor gave him some methadone to drink then and there, as it had been a few days since he'd had any. He may have given him a straw to use. David took a drink but, as much as he needed it, as much of a journey as it had been for him to get there, it all immediately came up through his nose. As I remember it, he looked confused for a moment, and then just kind of smiled, as if to say, *No harm done.*

In my notes about the trip, I wrote something about how he didn't want to go home—he wanted to stay in the taxi and keep driving and looking around at the evidence of springtime, but we didn't do it. I felt terrible about having dragged him to the V.A. for no reason, and about being too tired to at least ask the taxi driver to take one more run around the block.

Once we got home, sitting silently in his wheelchair as I sat wordlessly and dispiritedly beside him, David reached over and took my hand. I suppose he was thanking me for trying.

We must have sat like that, holding hands, for a long time, because I know that I wouldn't have wanted to let go.

Permission

One of my blog posts, written many years later, was this:

Every so often I find a sick or dying bird on a sidewalk somewhere. When they're in that state, too weak or tired to be afraid of me, it's easy to pick them up and take them home. Very often they'll look up into my eyes for a moment as if they're trying to gauge what my intentions might be, and as if they're saying, Do whatever you're going to do; I've given up.

Every so often I can save one. More often, it's too late, and all I can do is hold the bird in my hands to keep it warm until it dies. It will doze in my hands for hours, occasionally waking with a start, trying, it seems, to look as if there's nothing wrong with it, trying to convince both of us that it's fine. Gradually, though, its eyes will close again.

There have been times when I thought that I prolonged a bird's life beyond the point where it should have ended. Thinking that I was giving comfort, I may have, in fact, made it suffer more.

I couldn't imagine letting go, but I know that at one point I forced myself to tell David that it was O.K.— that he could stop fighting, that I'd understand. I remember saying it as we sat together on the futon one night. David didn't answer; it was nearly impossible for him to speak at all by then. But something did change after that. He seemed relieved, somehow, and he started to let go of life. Telling him that was one of the things that I did right back then.

Holding Breath

In his last few weeks,   David rarely lay down any more. At night, he would sit up for hours, staring at the wall, or at the floor, often with that strange little smile on his lips, as if he was being told some wonderful secret. Sometimes I'd try to pull him down, because it worried me that he wasn't sleeping. Sometimes he'd resist. Other times he would lie down, but his legs wouldn't straighten out.

He spoke very little, and when he did, the words would come out unexpectedly, quietly, slowly, as if they'd been inside of him for a long time and were just coming to the surface.

He had two homecare attendants, one during the day, and one at night. Sometimes I'd sleep with David with the attendant present; it may have seemed strange but I was well past caring about how anything seemed.

Other nights I'd send the attendant home, and take care of David myself. There's one night in particular that was like a tunnel of dreams, a kind of final journey. I'd gone out to Delancey to buy some sheets for the hospital bed. When I got back to the apartment I sent the homecare attendant home, and I had a sip of David's methadone (which the VA had sent home with him but which he hadn't been drinking) so that I could sleep. That night, for some reason, we slept in the hospital bed, or, I should say, I slept. David sat up for most of the night, looking at the floor.

At some point during the night, David said, "I need." He stopped there.

"What do you need?" I asked him.

It took him a few moments to form the words. "I

101

need someone to hold my breath for me."

I think I understood what he meant, but I don't remember how I answered. Maybe I told him that I would. Maybe that's what I'm trying to do now, as I write.

This is a poem that I wrote about that night:

HOLDING BREATH

April dusk drained, while I was out,
Into your mouth, the black
Collapsing cave, your glottis ticking off
Last swallows of the day. You watched tides
Receding, patterns on the rug
Recounting dreams, frail fingers
Fingering cold fences
That held you in your bed.

Coming in with sheets
And pillows from Delancey, I smelled your skin
Beleaguered., tasting itself, falling
Away, the smell of fruit
Rotting in a bowl, unnaturally sweet.
The nurse dismissed, I prematurely lit the room
With candles against night.

Then night began, a shadow
Lapping in the shallow moments. Rats
And pigeons rustled, pestilent,
Trapped in walls; open windows lifted tongues,
Sending quiet cadenced prayers
To infiltrate God's monotone. Your eyes,
Slow fish, slid in wide ellipses
While I prepared us for the caterpillar ride
To dawn. By nine I lay
Against your back between the rails, your muteness
Sharp against murmurs from the street,

102

Against the muffled rush of breeze
Through pale fingers of new leaves. Hooded figures
Flickered and bowed
In gestures of atonement on the walls.

There was nothing to do
But wait. I lay you down. Sometime that night
Your whisper broke
An interval of sleep. I need,
You said. I waited while
You shook it from inside your head.
I need someone
To hold my breath for me.

That night
I never slept again,
Imagining you driving on some prairie road,
Your arm dancing in the wind outside the window
With the rhythm of a country song.
I warmed your back curved hard
Against sleep, passing the hours preparing
For the time that we had left.

Hallucination

Two days before he died, David told me about a hallucination he'd had. It was night; I was getting ready to go to sleep and the nurse, Margaret, was sitting in a chair near the bed, watching television. David was sitting, as he usually did, on the edge of the bed, rarely speaking because it was so difficult for him, or maybe because (as he'd told me after the last time he was in the hospital), he sometimes thought he was talking when he really wasn't. I was sitting next to him, and he said, "I thought I saw something."

It was hard to hear him so I lay down right next to him and said, "What? What did you see?"

"Something in the room...the other day."

"Here? In this room?"

"Yeah."

"What? What did you see?"

"I saw..."

"You saw what?"

"Something like a rape."

I was talking as quietly and gently as I could, so that we were both whispering. My hand was on his knee, I think.

"You saw someone raped?"

"Yes."

"No one was raped in here, hon." (I'd recently taken to calling him "hon", which was really unlike me but just came out naturally with him by then.) "Were you alone? Who else was here?" He shook his head, or shrugged.

"Who was raped?" No answer.

"Was it someone you knew? David. Did you know who was raped?"

Then he sort of smiled. "I don't know." But the smile made me think he knew.

104

Of course I wondered if it was me, but I didn't say so. He wouldn't say any more about it. It was terrible to think that he'd been sitting almost completely silent all those days, hallucinating rapes or whatever he thought he was seeing, thinking he was talking, probably aware that he was hallucinating and that it was because his brain was being eaten into by lesions. I told him that the hallucinations would stop if he took his medications, and he seemed to believe it.

The last crime I would have imagined that David might hallucinate was a rape (or whatever "something like a rape" might have been). It didn't frighten me. He had never given me any reason to be afraid of him.

The next night I told Margaret about it in the kitchen, and she took it as an omen of some kind. She was really frightened, but I couldn't tell whether she thought a rape had really taken place or whether she believed that David was foreseeing something. I tried to calm her down by telling her that no one could get into the apartment, and that even if David had the strength to do so much as stand up on his own, he would never do either of us any harm. She kept saying that this would be her last job, and that she was going to request that a man replace her on the night shift.

Ambulance, and the Broken Promise

Just after he died, I started to record everything that I could remember about the last few days of David's life in the journal I'd been neglecting, in the obsessive fear that I'd forget the details. Finding it again years later, it was hard to read about one of my biggest mistakes—breaking my promise to David that I would not, under any circumstances, bring him back to the hospital:

I was exhausted, as I'd been every night, and went to bed at 9:30 or 10, even though the lights and television were on and David was still refusing to lie down. When I got into bed I lay with my back against David's, as he'd always liked me to do. I fell asleep quickly, and I don't remember waking up during the night.

At about five in the morning I woke up for some reason. David, who was still sitting on the edge of the futon, must have made some movement. I knew immediately that something was going to happen.

David started to fall slowly back onto the bed. I jumped up, calling for Margaret, who had fallen asleep on the hospital bed.

(Just now I remembered something that Margaret had said after I told her about the hallucination: "Most people with AIDS don't have the luxury of having someone sleep in the same bed with them." And then of something David had said months before, while we were walking up Houston: "Most junkies don't have the luxury of feelings." That he should have had to consider those things luxuries...I wonder what would have happened if I hadn't been there and Margaret had slept through the seizure. Would David have died at home that morning, in peace, with no spinal tap or needles?)

Margaret got up and looked at David and then at me, and I knew that she didn't know what to do either. David was lying on his back, twitching slowly, and his left arm had bent up toward his chest and twisted. His eyes were wide open and his irises were moving back and forth, unseeing. I thought that he would die at any moment, and I was afraid of him. I put a pillow under his head, terrified of touching him, and called 911. I was crying and shaking, but able to give all the information they needed on the phone. They told me to take the pillow out, and I did. I keep wondering now if I let his head down gently enough.

Margaret went outside to wait for the ambulance. All I could do was stand a little distance away from the bed, watching David and sometimes trying to tell him that everything would be all right. He seemed almost peaceful, unafraid.

(What I was afraid of was death. I'd never watched anyone die, and I'd always been afraid to touch anyone who was dead, no matter how much I loved him or her.)

When we left the apartment, with David strapped into a chair that the paramedics carried, his head wrapped in a blanket so that only his eyes showed through shadow, I picked up David's keys and my own and looked around and said goodbye to the apartment and our life together, because I knew for certain this time that it was over. My body was shaking and my teeth were chattering and I kept making ironic little jokes to Margaret because I didn't know what else to say. I left the apartment wearing the green pinstripe hospital robe that we'd stolen from the V.A. Hospital the last time David was discharged.

In the ambulance David was no longer spasmodic and Margaret and I sat side by side next to where he lay. I kept stroking his forehead, pushing his hair back with my palm as I'd always done, using the pretense of checking him for fever when I really just wanted to touch him. The skin on his forehead, like it had been all over his body before he really got sick, was smooth, and his hair was soft and fine. Later, when I did it again in the emergency room, I remarked how cold he felt and the nurse told me that his temperature was only 95 degrees.

107

When we started to move the paramedic sitting at David's head said something about DNR orders. It then occurred to me that David would want to die at home, and that we'd reached an unspoken agreement that I wouldn't take him to the hospital. I asked the paramedic if we could take him back home, but he only smiled, thinking, I suppose, that I was kidding.

The ride seemed quick. Margaret and I got out of the ambulance first and I was crying again because I thought I was betraying David and because that might be the last thing he thought of me. We were behind Bellevue and the sky over the East River was beginning to get light through a little rain. I turned to watch them take David out and Margaret said, "Stop crying now because he's looking at you." He was, in a calm, slightly uncomprehending way. His eyes looked huge and beautiful, and I wanted to tell him to turn and look at the sky over the river. My hand was over my mouth but I took it away and tried to stop crying and to look as if there was no reason to be afraid for him.

E.R.

The entry continued:

In the emergency room I was suddenly furious at everything. A patient was screaming, over and over, "Oh Jesus oh Mama please help me JESUS!" and I just wanted him to shut up.

A nurse asked me questions while they took David behind a curtain in the corner. I was really crying then, asking if I could just take him home because I'd promised that I wouldn't let him die in a hospital. Somehow I remembered his birthday, Medicaid number, Social Security number, and most of the medications he was supposed to be taking.

After a while they let me go to him. The doctor wanted me to hold his hands when they put an I.V. into his groin. I kept talking to him and telling him I was sorry and that I was trying to get them to let him go home. The doctor said that he probably had too much methadone and morphine in his system and that they were giving him something to counteract the effects. She said that it would make him lucid enough to talk (which I couldn't believe), and that if he was able to say for himself that he wanted to go home they might be able to let him.

After a few minutes he seemed to notice that I was holding his hands and he looked at me and said, "What are you doing here?" I was astonished. I told him where he was and what had happened and that he had to tell the doctor that he wanted to go home. He was perfectly lucid and kept asking me to help him get up. When the doctor came back I asked him again what he wanted to do. Margaret, on the other side of the bed, was asking him too. Everyone was talking at once, and again I asked him, for the doctor to hear, if he wanted to leave or stay. Margaret said something and David said, "Shut up"—which was utterly out of character for him but I think he just understood how important it was for him to be heard—so that I almost laughed and then he pulled my hands toward him and leaned up toward me and said, "I want to go with you." I smiled at him and the doctor said she'd go speak to the administrator about it.

A little later the nurses moved David to the other side of the room. Margaret said to David, "We were so worried about you, David. You had a seizure. You scared us." Motioning to me, she said, "She was crying." David looked at me and reached his hand out to me and I took it. Margaret said, "See? He's being so sweet to you," but David said, "Help me get up, please." I asked him to be patient a little longer; we didn't want anything to happen to him before they let him go. Next to us, behind a curtain, the man was still screaming, "Oh Jesus Jesus Mama Jesus!" I told David that the man was driving me crazy, but he said, "It's alright."

I left the room for a little while to make some calls, and by the time I got back David was starting to drift off again. The administrator came and asked him if he knew where he was and he said, "Bellevue." She talked to him a little more and agreed that he seemed rational, but said that there could be legal problems if they let him go. She went to call the V.A. to confirm that he'd had DNR orders there. I was getting nervous because David was almost asleep again, and, because I was neither his wife nor a relative, my word meant nothing. I was wondering if there was a way we could get married. I already felt like I was his wife.

By the time a new doctor came around David was sleeping and unresponsive again. The doctor was brusque and acted as if he didn't know that David had said he wanted to be discharged. I told him that he'd said it just a few minutes before. The doctor said that if David had signed DNR orders they would have been able to honor his wishes. I said, "He could have done that just a little while ago," but the doctor told me that it was "water under the bridge." It looked as if they were going to admit him no matter what happened.

Eventually I had to go to work. I walked to my mother's apartment in the hospital robe, a sweater, and a pair of shoes. Andy, David's daytime homecare worker, called me later from

110

the hospital to tell me that they'd admitted David, and that
they were going to give him a spinal tap. That, I knew, was
about the worst thing they could do to him. I wondered if he was
blaming me.

This is the last poem I wrote about David, in 1995
or 1996:

E.R., BELLEVUE, 4/20/90

It worked, whatever
They gave you, for five
Minutes, miracles. For five minutes
A pair of jack-o'-lantern flames
Flooded the hollowed crescents of your eyes, found
Me, fixed. Blues and whites ghosted by;
Metals in the room hummed frigid wiry songs.

It was a shot you could have popped
Yourself, two months, or less,
Before, fingers and limbs obeying brain. You knew
your name was David
Then. Your throat could swallow anything.

My mistake, your being there,
Your one request, to be at home, forgotten
When your sudden spasm woke me, the nervous
marbles
Of your irises colliding
With the curved-edged razors of your lids.
A filling-station fear of death in deep-
Night solitude made me betray you, make the call
To have them come and bring you in.

The ambulance threw fire down streets
And ran against crosslights, and heaved your head
From side to side, and would not

Turn around again.
Orange suns crashed into asphalt
When you were carried out, and clouds
Behind you shook. A yellow moon, your face
Swung over the misting river, against
A whitening sky. Neon flashed, arresting in red
Your last uncertain movements in fresh air. I
thought
I asked you something then, and thought you
answered
By the way that your expression
Didn't change.

Double doors breathed us in,
Exhaled the morning wind.
Patients turned their heads to watch it go.
Reciting all your numbers, all the thirty pills
I'd tried to make you take each day, infections,
Hospitalizations, whereabouts of kin,
I impressed the nurse who tied you to a bed.
Beyond that, being neither wife
Nor mother, sister, cousin once
Removed, it didn't matter what I said.
The answer had to come from you, and you
Had put the riches that remained inside your rusted
tin away
Two weeks ago, your mouth accepting morphine,
Nothing else. There's method
To my madness, you murmured once, your tongue
Arced up to take it in. From then you spoke
At intervals spaced out like stars
Against a stretched, black sky.

So you got your one
Last shot. Your veins, frayed wires,
Remembered, sent adrenaline up

112

Into your dark rooms
Which lit in sequence fast as Christmas bulbs,
And for five minutes glowed.

Asked, repeated, the question passed
From voice to voice in rounds, a chorus
In the cubicles and curtains.
I saw you register what I'd done, saw
The answer rise through levels to your mouth,
Saw you shape it with your lips, breathe:
I want to go with you,
But the voices by then were gone,
And you would not be going home.

Five Roses, and a Little Miracle

The story continued with what happened when I came back to the hospital after work that day:

I came back in the early evening. David was on the AIDS ward in a room with two other men. His bed was next to the window, but he lay on his back with his face turned toward the door. I think his eyes were open when I came in, but it was hard to tell if he realized that I was there. An I.V. was still in his groin. The doctors were trying to counteract his dehydration.

Before going into the room I'd spoken to his doctors—a woman and two men. I liked and trusted them almost immediately. They said they'd spoken to David's mother that morning. (I'd called her from work to tell her what had happened, and to ask her to call the hospital to request that David be put on DNR status. When I told her that that was what he wanted, she'd agreed immediately.) I was furious when the doctors told me that she'd told them to do everything possible to keep David alive until she got there the following afternoon. The doctors agreed with me, but said they could do nothing about it unless David became lucid again and asked to be allowed to die himself. They told me to come and get them if David started talking again.

David's room seemed huge and bare and the whole ward was very quiet. The window faced the Empire State Building and a gray dusk. In the bed next to David's was an emaciated black man who was nearly as still and silent as David. The other patient in the room was sitting up reading and looked relatively healthy. I smiled at him as I walked in, and he smiled back.

I'd brought David five red roses and I put them in a water pitcher on the table next to the window, assuming that he would eventually turn the other way and see them. As it turned out, he never did, as far as I know.

When I sat down next to the bed David was looking at me, and I knew that he knew that I was there. I tried talking to

114

him a little, very quietly, but he didn't respond. His right hand was under the sheet, covering the place where the I.V. went in. I tried to see if the ring that I'd given him was still on his finger, but I couldn't see and David seemed to resist when I tried to move his hand. I told him that I only wanted to see if the ring was still there, and maybe hold it for him until he got out. I don't know exactly why it seemed so important, except that I wanted to wear it after he died. I'd always thought of it as a kind of secret wedding ring. Maybe he thought of it the same way; I don't know. I'd given it to him to replace another ring that I'd given him months before, which had apparently slipped off of his finger because he'd lost so much weight. The first ring was silver, two dolphins circling his finger and facing each other. I think he'd liked the first one more. When I gave him the second one, after yelling at him for about twenty minutes because he hadn't gone to a clinic appointment, he dropped it and suddenly started to sob. I'd put my arm around his shoulder and my head on his collarbone while he cried, and after a while I picked the ring up off of the floor and put it on his finger.

"...which had apparently slipped off of his finger because he'd lost so much weight." Writing that, I must have known that that was not the case, that he'd given away or traded the first ring. Either that, or I desperately needed to believe something else at that moment.

I've wondered for a long time what it was that made David cry on that day when I gave him the second ring; I was afraid that I'd never thought to ask him, or to say anything that might have helped, or that he'd told me and I'd forgotten, or that I'd just been too harsh in yelling at him about the appointments. I wondered if it might have been that he didn't want to wear the ring. But now I think I know what it was. He was standing by the bed, sobbing, with the new ring on the floor and my head on his shoulder, and after a few minutes he said. "I don't know who I am anymore." (I believe that that was also when he said, "You know, when I was in the hospital the first time and I had a lot of time to think, I decided to get rid of all the bad things in my personality.")

I wish that I'd known to suggest to him that perhaps "not knowing who he was anymore" meant that something good was in the process of happening—that he was gradually losing the armor that he'd been using to protect himself, and the blind drive to anesthetize himself, that had for so long kept the sweetness in him from shining as it should. It must have been painful, like regaining the feeling in a limb that had been asleep for a very long time, and yet knowing that he would have very little time left to use it again.

The story continues:

After a while I stopped talking and just sat with my hand on David's arm, leaning over the metal rail on his bed. Sometimes I looked at his eyes, which were usually looking at me. At one point I started to cry, quietly, and I looked toward the window. I think David noticed, because he moved a little and when I looked at him his lips moved, and I'm almost certain that they formed the words, "I love you." We sat and stared at each other, and I had a feeling that we were coming to an understanding and I loved him even more, and I smiled as if we were actually speaking. His eyes were calm and beautiful and kind, and I wanted to get into the bed and lie down with him and stay with him until he died.

Did he say that? I can see his mouth moving, even now, but not clearly enough to tell. Even then, sitting there with him in that silent room with tears on my face, I couldn't be sure, and I know my propensity to remember things as I wanted them to be, and not necessarily as they were.

If that was what he was trying to tell me, it was a final act of kindness, and something that, even then, I

116

wasn't able to do myself. He was barely able to move at all, and thinking, at times, that he was speaking when he wasn't, and no doubt aware, when he was aware of anything, that he could die at any moment. Telling me that he loved me would do him no good, and would require an expense of an energy that was quickly leaving him of its own accord. If that was what he was doing, he was doing it only because he knew at that point that I needed to hear it.

I continued:

I left after a while and told David I'd be back in an hour or two. A nurse gave me permission to get an overnight pass, so I went home to change and came back at around eight. David was asleep when I came in, so I sat and ate a bagel and read the paper.

At about nine I pulled two chairs together and lay down, using my sweater as a pillow. David hadn't said anything. Nurses occasionally came in to check on his I.V., and they were all very kind to me. They probably assumed that I was his wife. I drifted in and out of strange half-dreams, because I'd taken some morphine that day to help me calm down and because the chairs weren't very comfortable. Once I went out into the hall to ask for a glass of water. I was barefoot, and one of the security guards told me that I should be wearing shoes. Then he asked me what I was in the hospital for. Another guard told him that I was a visitor, not a patient.

In the very early part of the morning, while it was still dark, I heard a nurse come in and say hello to David. I lifted my head and started to say that he wasn't talking, when I heard his voice say, "Hi," very clearly. Amazed, I got up and went to him. I asked him how he felt and he said O.K., but he wanted some water. A nurse went to get him some, and I held it for him while he drank it through a straw.

I said, "Do you know where you are?" and he said that he was in the hospital, but he didn't know which one. I told him. He said he didn't remember anything about the seizure so I told

117

him a little about it. One of the nurses in the room said to him, "Someone's happy that you're talking." It was true; while they took his temperature I was practically dancing around the room.

When the nurses left I went back to helping David drink. He was very thirsty. I told him that they were letting me spend the night with him, and that I was sleeping right behind him. He looked surprised, and tried a little to look behind him. As he was drinking I figured that I probably wouldn't have much time to get him to tell someone that he wanted DNR status. I still regret saying it: "David. This is important. You have to tell the doctor that if you stop breathing you don't want them to put you on a machine." As I said it he fell asleep again. I hope it wasn't the last thing he remembered me saying.

I went to sleep again, but a doctor came in and woke me up. He said that he wanted to take some blood from David, and that so far the tests they'd done had shown nothing more than toxoplasmosis. He asked me to hold David's arm while he took the blood. I was amazed that he was able to find a vein in the arm, because no one had even tried to do that in months. David didn't move, but he held my hand very tightly so I stood with him for quite a while. The doctor was so gentle and concerned that I practically fell in love with him too. I wished that he could have been David's doctor all along, and I said, "See, David? We've found a miracle doctor who can find veins in your arms." The doctor said that it was because David was so thin, but he'd been thin for a very long time.

After testing the blood the doctor came back in and said that everything looked pretty good. David was in no immediate danger. We talked about what would happen when David's mother and brother arrived, and I told him that I might have to be restrained. He said, "Oh, good. Then it will be a real circus in here." We laughed. I explained that I was angry because David's family hadn't seen him in ten or twelve years, and now they were suddenly concerned and interfering with David's wishes. We agreed that we could understand their wanting to see him alive, but that it seemed cruel. The doctor said, "You've *been with him through all of this?" and I said yes. I thanked him several times before he left, and then went back to sleep.*

To this day I still think that that doctor was some kind of angel—whatever an angel is.

The entry continued:

I woke up early. It was raining outside. David's head felt hot, and he wasn't responsive at all. After drinking some coffee I told him that I was going to my mother's apartment to have a nap and a shower, and that I'd be back in a few hours. He still hadn't turned his head (although I'd tried to move it during the night, it seemed stuck in that position), and he was looking in my direction as I left the room. I don't think he really saw me, though.

I read this, and I still can't understand why I left that morning. The shower could have waited, and sleep, at that point, wasn't important. What the hell was I thinking? The only possible reason I can come up with sounds ridiculous in retrospect, but I know myself well enough to think that it is in all likelihood the real one. I wanted to go home and clean up and put on some makeup and the blue dress that David seemed to love to see me wear. I wanted to look nice for him.

The Oarless Boat

In my journal, I found this account of what happened when I returned to the hospital:

I'm home. I'm on an ocean in an oarless boat. I don't understand why he didn't wait. I told him I'd be back, that I was just going home for a little while to rest and take a shower.

I came in clean, rested, dressed for him, smiling at the nurses. One of them blocked my way in the hall, holding out her hand. I thought she was trying to introduce herself, but she pulled her hand away when I reached for it and put it on my shoulder and told me. She sat me down and said that the doctor would be up soon to take me to him.

The doctor didn't come and I made the nurses take me to the room. The curtain had been pulled around his bed, but everything was very bright, and quiet. There was a lot of white—the white sheets, tangled around him in places, kicked off in others, white light on his pale skin, white walls, the whites of his eyes. His irises had rolled up back into his head; the beautiful darkness was gone, leaving two white pools of nothing. There was something obscene about the way he'd been left there, barely covered, his eyelids left open like that. He hadn't died peacefully; he looked as if he'd been fighting demons. I was afraid to touch him, or go too near.

The nurses left me there with him, and I sat by the window in one of the chairs I'd slept in the night before and watched him. His face was turned away from me. In my mind I was trying to pray and say things to him and say things to myself, all at the same time. The words tangled around each other and lost meaning and got louder in my head, competing with each other as if three people were talking to me at once, each trying to be heard above the other two. I looked at Sam's chest to see if it was moving. After a while the doctor came in. "It's only the girlfriend," someone said, and the doctor left again.

120

The nurses came back and asked me to leave so that they could do whatever it is they do. I said, "There's a ring on his hand that I gave him." One of them pulled the sheet back and lifted his hand, but the ring was on his stomach. I didn't remember it being loose enough to come off by itself. She handed it to me and I put it on, as I'd imagined myself doing even as I bought it.

They seemed to think I was in the way. For a while I walked through the halls, looking for someone I recognized. I passed a chaplain, but Sam would have wanted nothing to do with him. Everything was quiet, dull, unimpressed by what had happened. In the sunroom I sat by the window looking down at the river and straight out at the silver threads of rain straining at an angle from the clouds to the earth and water. I was trying not to think about what they were doing to him or where they would take him, or about how things would be from now on, or how they could have been, or about how he might have thought I let him down. Boats on the river were disappearing into fog in both directions, and to stay calm I picked out the slowest one and counted in my head until I couldn't see it any more.

Nothing happened for a long time and it occurred to me that there was no reason for me to stay. I was afraid that if I left without telling anyone they might send Sam to the morgue and then to Potter's Field, thinking that no one would have made other plans for him. I went back to his room and the bed was empty. The five red roses I brought him yesterday were still on his table, so I took them and went to the nurses' station and asked if there was anything I needed to do. At first they looked at me as if they didn't know who I was and then someone said that Sam would be in the morgue until arrangements were made for a funeral. I said thank you, and left.

No one looked at me as I walked down First Avenue with the roses held in front of me. The rain had stopped and I could smell the earth and the river. Clouds in the south were pulling away from each other and behind them slid a thin strip of blue.

121

I was angry because the spring we'd been waiting for, the real spring that led without false starts to summer, seemed to begin as soon as I got outside. We always expected to at least have summer together.

I came home and got into bed again because I didn't know what else to do. The windows were closed but as I fell asleep I could hear muted sirens going past. I dreamed that I was back in Sam's room again, standing by the window in gray light. He was still alive and still motionless, facing the door. I took a few steps toward him and then woke up because he started to die. Muscles twitched erratically all over my body as if something was under my skin, panicking, trying to get out.

Maybe he had waited too long already, or maybe he wanted to do this last thing by himself, without my help or interference. Maybe he wanted to spare me seeing it, knowing that I'd never seen anyone die, but I'd always planned to be with him when it happened. Maybe it had nothing to do with anyone but him.

It's almost night. I have no idea how to spend all the time that still has to pass.

After all those months during which we were so alone together, with only each other to rely on, after my promise (perhaps unspoken, because it would have been so hard to talk about, but nevertheless understood by both of us) that I would never leave him alone again, that I would be there until his breathing stopped for good, I wasn't there at that last moment. The knowledge tormented me. It was terrible to believe that I would never even be able to explain to him that it was only because of a stupid mistake, and not because I'd panicked and deserted him at the last minute, that he died alone.

I think I wrote this the day after David died, as I waited out the morning and long afternoon in the apartment on Suffolk Street. Even then, I persisted in calling him "Sam"; even at that point I was apparently afraid of being found out:

Embarrassing, this morning, to find things where I left them last night, as if I'd gone to bed drunk, blacked out, woke up remembering the mess I'd made of everything in my delirium. Everything as it had been, familiar, defiant, caught in the process of separating itself from me, sidestepping sentimentality.

On my table, in a pitcher I took from the hospital, the roses, blown open during the night as far as they'd go before falling apart. Your boots on the floor, size twelve but not nearly big enough for your swollen feet since February. Thrown over an armchair, the dress you chose every time I asked you what I should wear. I put it on again, touched nothing else, and took the bus down here. It was the Avenue A to Houston, a ride I've taken so often that today I couldn't feel the horror of it.

Your radio was still on. I could hear it from the hallway. I half-expected to find the apartment ransacked, left bare and sunless, noisy with rats no longer frightened back deep into the walls by your stick or my fist on the floor. Or to find you still sitting, silent, on the bed or in your wheelchair with the T.V. on, aware of nothing but whatever it was that you watched in the pattern of the rug. But everything is the same as it was when they carried you out at dawn with a blanket wrapped around your head and shoulders so that only your eyes showed through shadow.

Now I'm sitting on the bed in an irregular square of sunlight that's moving gradually away from me toward the stain on the edge of the bed where you sat up every night and day for a week and a half, refusing to lie down for more than half an hour at a time except for the night your mind went completely and I didn't know it until morning when I woke and turned to you and you were staring at me but seeing nothing. It was the night that I was afraid of you for the first and only time. We didn't have a nurse for you yet and I'd been sleeping, worn out from watching you, next to where you sat. You were completely still, as you usually were, but an hour or two after midnight I must have heard you moving because I woke up and asked you what you were doing. You were leaning far over your knees and picking

123

at the thigh of your jeans as if you were trying to pull a string off of it, except that there was no string. You said, "I'm trying to clean myself off." I ran my hand lightly up and down your back a few times and asked you why and you answered, "I have to clean myself off a little. I can smell myself," and I could smell it too and I knew that you'd wet yourself and I remembered how you used to say that you didn't want to end up pissing all over yourself all the time and having to wear diapers like an infant or old man. Quietly I asked you to lie down and get a little sleep and I told you that I'd give you a bath in the morning. You didn't answer so I pulled you down toward the pillow and I was surprised because you let me. You lay on your back but your legs wouldn't straighten out and I told you to concentrate and relax them and you said you couldn't. In the dark I pulled and massaged them until they released and straightened. Then I said goodnight and became afraid, thinking that later in the night you might not know who I was, that your fear of strangers in your house might give you strength to hurt me as I slept. But your breathing slowed and became even and I knew that you were finally sleeping and so I slept too, not waking until morning when I found that you didn't know what anything was any more.

I've opened the windows and I can hear the hushed roar of approaching summer, made up of leaves brushing together and wind pushed aside by cars and voices blocks away. When you first started to get really sick and went into the hospital for the second time and I was here alone at night it sometimes seemed as if you were already gone. I'd sit and listen to the quiet inside and to the distant noises from the streets until I couldn't stand it any more and I'd have to turn the T.V. or the radio on, loud.

This is a good bed and I don't know what to do with it. I can't keep it and I don't want anyone else to have it. There probably aren't many people who would want it anyway, because you're dead, because you had AIDS, because you were an addict and people seem to think that those things are

124

somehow contagious by vague associations, or simply reasons to hate who you were. But I didn't catch anything and this bed, more and more, became the center around which we orbited, the safe place, the place where at first we hoped and, later, where we waited.

On a Sunday like this people are out buying the Times, *having brunch, walking. If you were here I would have gotten up at about eight to have coffee and a bath. At ten or eleven, if you weren't already awake, I'd have knelt down next to you and brushed your hair away from your forehead with my hand until you woke up. You'd have had your methadone and put on a shirt, and we'd have gone over to the Dominican restaurant on Essex for breakfast. Junkies would have been standing around outside the Essex Market, and you would have taken pleasure in telling me who they were and how they were working things.*

The square of light has slipped over the end of the bed onto the floor. I expected to be out of here before dark, but this still seems to be the safest place to be.

Aside from writing that, I don't know what else I did that day. I don't think I did anything at all, except sit on the bed and watch the sunlight from that beautiful April day move, once last time, slowly across the room. It seems to me that it was that afternoon that I said a silent prayer to him to find a way to come back to me if he ever could.

When it started to get dark I called my friend Joe, who drove into the city to pick me up and take me back to Hoboken, carrying David's jacket and boots, and a couple of his shirts. No doubt he gave me Calvados, good food made from groceries he'd bought at Balducci's, and sensible conversation.

Errands, and the Service

The tasks relegated to the living in the aftermath of a death are, on the surface, so mundane and trivial that if you allow yourself the luxury of being absent-minded as you do them they might seem to be of no greater significance than going to the post office, picking up the cleaning, doing taxes, choosing flowers for a dinner party. Within the week or so after David died, I made several trips to Redden's funeral home on Fourteenth Street to sign forms, make a deposit, specify cremation over burial, and plan a modest memorial service. The City of New York would pay $900 toward after-death expenses; this basically covered disposing of the body in one way or another. My mother helped me pay for the rest, and I'll always be grateful for that.

In the evenings, after work, I had no choice but to get used to going home alone to my own apartment again. I think that I was still too stunned to feel much pain, and there was no one, even among my friends, with whom I could be completely honest about what had happened, and what I felt. I tried going out once or twice to my old hangouts, but I could only sit, silent and unable to relate to anyone around me, before giving up and coming home to smoke, write, have some wine or a sip of the last of David's methadone, listen to music (the Cowboy Junkies, Patsy Cline, K.D. Lang, Crazy Horse) and think about David and where he was. It was a muted version of the utterly out-of-control, full-blown, resurrected grief that felt as if it would kill me, sixteen years later.

I also had to make a trip out to an office in Brooklyn to pick up David's death certificate, and go shopping in the city for an outfit for him to "wear" at the service. The latter was, of course, the most surreal of the tasks; I had to pick out a button-down shirt, a tie, and a pair of slacks—none of which he'd had any use for in life, at least not lately—all the while making educated guesses as to the sizes he'd need, and the colors he might like.

Somehow I got in touch with David's vet friends and invited them to the service, and I enlisted some of my own friends, and my mother, to attend too. I wanted the room provided by the funeral home for the service to be as full as possible. David had already gone through dying alone.

In my journal, I wrote:

There is something obscene about this, not vaguely distasteful, but truly grotesque. Look at what I've done: on Monday I left work early to shop for clothes for a man four days dead, a man who while he was alive usually couldn't afford to buy himself a pair of socks, to wear to his funeral. All up and down Fourteenth Street, among the racks and shelves of bargains at Robbin's and American Value Center and the men outside yelling, "Todo bueno, todo barato." *I walked, and I imagined that Sam was there, behind and a little above me, protesting my selections, scowling at the security guards who looked at my bags as I left the stores to see if I had stolen anything.*

I dropped the clothes off at the funeral home as if I was leaving them at the hospital for a friend who was getting ready to go home, and went back to my apartment to get dressed for the memorial service.

When I came back, no one had arrived yet. John, the funeral director, led me to the room where the service was to be held, and left me there. At one end of the room was the casket and the pot of long forsythia branches that Joe and his girlfriend had left in the morning. Facing it were five or six rows of wooden chairs, and there was a guest-book on a table by the door. I'd been thinking that the service would just happen, take shape of

127

*its own accord, and when I realized that nothing would happen
without my making it happen I felt more lonely and afraid that
I had after coming home alone when Sam died. It was a rented
room set up for a show, and there would be an audience and one
performer. Sam would be the prop.*

*I avoided looking at him for a few minutes but it seemed rude
so I walked as quietly as I could over to the casket…*

The page that follows is lost; perhaps that's for the
best. I remember well enough how he looked.

There were nine people at David's memorial service,
including me. According to the guest book, Richie
and Robin were there, along with another one of
David's vet buddies. Joe came with his girlfriend, and
one of my best friends from work came with her
girlfriend. Another close friend from work, Bill, came
alone. My mother was there, too.

Robin read an eloquent eulogy, and I read a
Chippewa poem I'd somehow found:

> *A loon*
> *I thought it was.*
> *But it was*
> *My love's*
> *Splashing oar.*
> *To Sault St. Marie*
> *He has departed.*
> *My love*
> *He has gone on before me.*
> *Never again*
> *Can I see him.*

That was as far as I'd ever gone in admitting to
anyone what it was that I really felt for David.

At the end, Richie and Robin surprised me by folding a flag into the triangle shape used in military funerals, and presented it to me.

There was a big pot of flowers near the casket. Toward the end of the service, it tipped over for no discernible reason. I think it had everyone a little spooked. It crossed my mind for a moment that it was David who had knocked the pot over, and that he was trying to tell me that he was angry, or just asking us not to leave him there alone. But it was just an offhand thought; as much as I may have wanted to believe in spirits just then, I really didn't. If I had, I would have undoubtedly stayed in the room until the last possible moment.

But it was a nice service. David would have been pleased. At least I hope so, after everything else that had happened.

At work, I pulled out David's file and wrote "DECEASED" on it, and put it in the "Inactive" section of the file cabinet, as I'd done with so many other files in the past.

Looking for Him

It was strange, having nowhere to go but home to my apartment in Hoboken at the end of the day. The warm, early spring continued, and I would get home from work, perhaps have something to eat, and spend the evening writing, or just sitting and listening to music or watching television. My clearest memory of that time is the way the old elm and maple trees outside my bedroom windows rustled in the evening breeze and made delicate, ephemeral shadows on the walls, whispering to me until I fell asleep. Every few nights I'd have another quarter-capful of one of the bottles of methadone that David had never been able to use, and have peaceful, vivid dreams.

The movie *Ghost* had just come out; I didn't see it at the time but, although I knew that it was stupid to do so, I cried whenever I saw the advertisements for it on T.V.

Late one weekend morning I stepped outside my front door and saw a bird sitting at the top of my stoop, looking at me. It wasn't one of the pigeons, or sparrows, or grackles that came around all the time; it was a nondescript gray bird. As far as I could tell, it wasn't sick or injured, but it stood by the door and watched me without fear, and didn't fly away for a long time. I wasn't in any frame of mind that would make me think that it didn't have something to do with David.

On April 29th, a few days after the memorial service, I went out to Long Island and wrote this:

I'm at the house in Hampton Bays, and it's a chilly, damp day. It's been two days since I had any of David's leftover morphine or methadone and I'm experiencing no symptoms of withdrawal, only the edginess of my natural, undrugged self and occasionally the sorrow and frustration of reaching with my heart or mind for David, making a plan for us or thinking of something to say to him, and remembering over and over that he's not there on Suffolk Street, or in the hospital, or anywhere I can find him. There is no one I can talk to, because no one knows about death and what happens after and no one can tell me whether David can or will visit me in one form or another if I wait patiently enough, or summon him desperately enough. No one can tell me if he's waiting for me, or whether he might be waiting for someone other than me, or no one at all. Or if death really means that there's nothing to anyone any more.

I have summoned him. So far nothing definitive has happened. The pot of blossoming branches fell over at the funeral after having remained upright all day, but no doubt they were disturbed after the casket was opened so that I could see David. Once or twice, when I was ready to smash glass through glass or wood down through anything and the tears started, after a whole week, to come, my hand lifted and I stared at it and saw a pulse in it and stared for so long that peace came, and I felt warm as if his body was wrapped around my back and shoulders the way I used to wrap myself around him at night when he was cold or too unsteady to even lie down.

About a week after David's memorial service, Redden's called me to let me know that I could come in and pick up his ashes. I walked over on my lunch break. It was hot, and sunny, and I was surprised how heavy the box was. I carried it back to work in a plastic bag, as if I'd gone shopping on Fourteenth Street, and it sat on my desk for the rest of the afternoon, until it was time to go home. A day or two later, I went out to my mother's house in Hampton Bays. I wrote this on May 10th:

Everything except the ashes has been done. None of it was all that different from how I'd imagined it, planned it, all along, except that a few more people came to the service than either of us had expected, that the ashes were heavier than I

Description

This, written in early May as I contemplated the dull black plastic box that held David's ashes, is a very difficult one of the fragments for me to read, because it leaves no doubt that he had told me a great deal about the abuse he'd been subjected to as a child (one of the things about which I had, for some reason, completely forgotten until I heard about it again many years later), and about the shame he'd been made to feel:

Bones, brain, liver, bowels, eyes, limbs. Blood and once-irregularly beating heart. Skin smooth as a six-year-old's until the night it began to flake and peel because everything he tried to eat had been coming out through his nose, disobeying gravity, overriding his body's mechanisms for feeding itself. Hair, branches and buds of forsythia, mortician's makeup, the shirt and tie and pants I bought so he could have something to wear when they laid him out. Dust of a body formed and neglected for 42 years, turned vengefully against itself in the last nine months, a gestation ending in death.

I've got him right here, the man who turned one cold cloudless afternoon as we sat in the sun on his bed as if to kiss me, who turned wordlessly and without reproach back when I panicked and did nothing, who came with me to pick out a puppy, who came, feverish, all the way to New Jersey one freezing night to be with me because the puppy had been killed. A man who took all manner of pills without discrimination all his life, who refused to take the ones that might prolong it. Fool. Liar. Thief. Guilt-maddened beaten child. Gentleman of faultless manners, kind when it was pointless.

I suppose that I was at the "anger" stage of grief at that point, and that, wrong as I knew it to be, I was blaming him for what had happened to him.

Pure

I don't know whether I believed that I was being honest when, in my first attempt at writing David's book, I wrote something about "Anne's" love for "Sam" being "pure, because it had nothing to do with their bodies." I don't remember feeling lust in the usual sense for David at the time (had I kissed him, though, that may well have changed), but I think that had more to do with the near-impossibility of the situation than with any lack of attraction. ("Safer sex" practices—and I did have what was probably the only job in which condoms were passed out as office supplies along with pens, papers, and manila folders—would have seemed even more distasteful to me than usual with him, because they would have served to make his sense of being a pariah even stronger, I think, than simply abstaining altogether. Of course, he may not have even had the strength to make love, even if we'd tried.)

We touched each other all the time, but always employed the conceit that we did it as friends giving physical comfort—just as, when we talked about somehow having a child together, we spoke as if I were merely a close friend who wanted something to remember him by after his death, and to give him the gift of knowing that something of him would live and be cared for. I know that I checked him for fever much more often than was necessary even for a man with AIDS, because the feel of the smooth skin of his forehead and his soft hair beneath my hand was something I kept craving. We sometimes held hands when we walked outside, and at night he would usually ask me to lay with my back flat against his, to keep it warm. Other times, when he was shaking with chills, I would wrap myself around his body to make the shaking stop. We rubbed each others' shoulders; he rubbed my feet. *He* rubbed *my* feet, although I'd never asked him to do it.

I do remember wishing sometimes that he would turn around in the middle of the night to hold me, all on his own, for no reason except a desire to hold me. But he never did; at the time, insecure as I was about how he felt about me, I thought it was because he didn't think about me that way. Of course, I was conveniently forgetting that he had tried to kiss me once, and that I had refused at the time, and that the meaning that he must have taken from that was that it was, in fact, me who didn't think of him that way, or perhaps that I didn't see him as worth the risk. We really were a very confused pair of people, in that respect.

But a dream I had in early May, several weeks after David's death, was a pretty good indicator that my feelings toward David were not nearly as "pure" as my alter-ego Anne imagined they were:

I was getting married, although I didn't even know who I was marrying and I didn't really want to. It just seemed that it was time, and that things would be easier on everyone if I did.

The wedding was to start soon, in a big, dark, modern church with many floors, like a stadium almost. I went looking for David. He was with his junkie-vet friends in a kind of amphitheater, which was lit only by the burning ends of their cigarettes and the glowing ashes on the floor. There were twenty or thirty men, most of whom I knew, and they were all sitting cross-legged on the floor, each in the center of a circle of embers. David was on the far end, and I went to him.

The next thing I remember is that a black man carrying a hose came in, saying that the place was on fire and that we all had to get out. Everyone left, and David and I were still trying to get out when the man turned on the hose, from which came flames. He was spraying the amphitheater with fire, row by row, and David and I were trying to get to the door. The man was spraying toward our feet, ignoring us when we told him to stop.

David turned to him to make him stop, and I heard the man hit him. He fell back toward me, and was lying on his back and I knelt over him, because there was something wrong with the way his eyes looked and I thought he was going to die. Suddenly we started to make love, even though I was about to get married and I knew that someone would be coming in at any time and I knew that it was dangerous. There was no way to stop, though. It was wonderful and terrifying, and I woke up.

In early May, just after I'd finally buried David's ashes and come home, my friend Lynn took me to her parents' beach cottage in Delaware for a few days. I was terrible company—I think that I was just starting to think of David as really gone—but she was patient with me, and just let me brood. Still, I think I held back, because I still felt like the unacknowledged, secret widow, the one with no right to grieve beyond the point prescribed for, say, a friend, or a client to whom I'd taken a particular liking. Lynn understood better than almost anyone else, but she still couldn't know exactly what it was that I'd lost.

I wrote this after a day spent watching the wild ponies on the island of Assateague, which I'd wanted to see since I was a little girl obsessed with the book *Misty of Chincoteague:*

It seems that everything that happens, or that I see, hear, or think about, will in one way or another refer back to or remind me of the time I spent with David. Particularly the beautiful things I'd imagined us seeing or doing together or things I imagined him doing before I met him, before he got sick, before he came to New York. He would have loved Assateague, and the country nearby, and the ponies. Today I walked up the beach a little and saw four ponies—three mares and a stallion,

I think—and the stallion (maybe because David is always in the back of my mind, especially today, for some reason, and because it seems that every few minutes something will start to make me ache inside and I'll realize that something has brought a memory of him back and I wonder how in eight months we'd accumulated so much that almost everything now makes me think of him) made me think of David. He was smaller and lighter in color than the other ponies, but he had an air that was devilish, wild, and gentle. I don't think that I was looking for a comparison; it just struck me and it took me a few minutes to realize what it was.

Lynn and I walked along a short trail through woods to the marshes, and I was wondering why I'd ever wanted to live in the city and why I couldn't have had just a few more weeks to get David out. So I cried a little, suddenly, surprisingly, as we left the island.

Maybe it was the dream about making love to David in the amphitheater that got me thinking about him like this.

So now I can't stop writing about everything because I have this consuming point of reference that intensifies every experience and I don't want to forget or lose anything.

Damn it's hard to be in love with someone who's dead because all I can do, it seems, is to love him more and more and he's not there to be real enough or human enough to temper it. And there's so much I thought we'd have time to settle, and so little that I paid enough attention to. I don't know if he died thinking of me as a friend, a lover, or a traitor.

With the exception of one last note scrawled on my list of things to remember, and the few poems and odd bits of writing that I did years later, that was the last thing I wrote about him, except for one final note, which reads:

--taking him with me wherever I go now

Interview

A month or so after David died, I got it into my head that I wanted to get a job as a counselor at the V.A. Hospital. I'm sure that somewhere inside myself I thought that I might be able to "find" David there again, to conjure up some piece of him to keep with me. And I'd certainly become familiar with the place.

The fact was that I was barely able to work at all, anywhere, but I had no choice but to try to make a show of it. Just as when David had been alive, and we would spend our time together talking about the places we'd go when we made our escape from New York, from his illness, his death sentence, I sat at home most evenings daydreaming about moving out to Montana or Wyoming, living alone or, when the time came, marrying some cowboy-type and forgetting everything about the past. God knows where I came up with that stuff, or why I thought it would be a solution to anything.

I don't even remember what my days were like, or how I managed to perform all the little bureaucratic tasks that my job required. I was undoubtedly even more useless than I'd been before.

Somehow, though, I managed to get a job interview at the V.A.. As if I weren't already in enough of a trance, I drank a little methadone before I went in. Clearly, whatever it was I was hoping to find there, it wasn't really a job; I knew perfectly well that the V.A. guys were no fools when it came to spotting someone who was high.

The "interview" was held in a big, gray conference room. I was invited to sit down at a table around which, as I remember it now, there seemed to be at least ten people, all of whom, to my bewilderment, seemed to know me, although I didn't recognize any of them. A lot of them seemed to be doctors and counselors.

"We know about what you did for David," someone was saying. I should have panicked then, but he continued—something along the lines of, "It was wonderful, and we just wanted to start out by letting you know that we recognize it, and appreciate it." It was as if they'd invited for the interview solely for the purpose of telling me that.

I still have no idea how they knew who I was, or what my relationship with David had been. Aside from a very few close friends knowing about it, we'd always felt alone and anonymous in the strange, beautiful little universe we'd created for ourselves. It must have occurred to me sometimes how incongruous with our surroundings we must have been together when we were away from Suffolk Street, and how odd I must have looked to the vets as I wheeled David through the halls at the hospital, or watched *Jeopardy* with the patients in the visitors' room there, or led the little parade up to the methadone clinic that spring day. What I hadn't considered was that in that small, insular world inhabited by veterans with drug addictions and AIDS, where very little happened or changed aside from people dying, we would have, of course, been talked about.

I was stunned; I can only imagine how idiotic I must have looked, dressed in my interview clothes, staring at them with my dead-giveaway red, glassy, small-pupiled eyes, trying to understand what was happening. I don't even know if we ever got to the interview itself.

The fact that they had thanked me for what I had "done for" David, as if I'd been able or had had any desire to do things differently, of course, meant that they had no more idea than anyone else how I'd thought of him; they probably would have never imagined that I would have the kinds of dreams I had about him, or the regrets about missed opportunities. But their kindness—especially because it told me that there had, in fact, been people other than me who had cared about and respected David—was an unexpected gift, at a time when I needed one.

When I left, the man who had first spoken to me shook my hand and said a very warm goodbye. They didn't hire me, of course. That would have been insane. In spite of what they thought about what I had "done for" David, they knew damn well that I was a train wreck, and would be for a long time.

PART THREE: EXCAVATING, DIVING, FINDING HIM AGAIN

There are so many layers to this story—layers of time and memory, layers of understanding, layers of grief and unexpected joy. Even now, every time I think that it's all finally reached its conclusion, something else happens, and I find myself revising the story once again.

After my first serious attempt to write a book about David, a couple of years after his death, I never really tried again. I simply didn't know how to do it, and I felt that I didn't understand nearly enough about him or about what had happened between us to keep trying. I wrote a few poems about him, but nothing more.

But after going through my journals for the first time in many years back in the summer of 2006, it occurred to me that I had at my disposal something that hadn't been available to me in the past—blogs. If nothing else, I thought, I could put as much as I could remember into a blog of my own, thereby assuaging some of the guilt caused by my broken promise to David. There would, I thought, be no pressure, and no time-limit, and I could just write what I felt comfortable writing. It would be, at least, a start.

The first few posts to the blog were fairly straightforward and at times almost flippant descriptions of David and how we'd met (what I could remember of it without having read more of my journals, letters, and other—at that point—lost bits of writing). What I didn't foresee was that once I started in earnest the necessary process of going back through those records, and layers and years of memory, I would be beginning an excavation of a part of myself that I had left all but untouched, an exercise in remembering that would within a couple of weeks send me into a period of grief that was deeper and blacker and more lonely than what I'd felt even in the first few weeks after David's death. It was the grief that I hadn't allowed myself back then, when no one save a few of my closest friends had any idea what it had meant to me to lose him, when I'd buried him alone.

Nor did I have any idea that there was a name for what I'd somehow believed was peculiar to me, and that, especially in the 1980's and early 1990's, there were many people who had found themselves in the same position. The term for it is "disenfranchised grief"; I don't remember how I came across the definition online, but reading it gave me, for the first time, an understanding that at least I wasn't alone in my transgression of the rules, and that I could perhaps at least start to forgive myself for prematurely laying my grief aside and moving on at the time:

Disenfranchised grief is the result of a loss for which they do not have a socially recognized right, role or capacity to grieve. These socially ambiguous losses are not or cannot be openly mourned, or socially supported. Essentially, this is grief that is restricted by "grieving rules" ascribed by the culture and society. The bereaved may not publicly grieve because, somehow, some element or elements of the loss prevent a public recognition.

Some of those "elements" might include a "relationship that is not socially recognized" (for example, partners in a lesbian or gay relationship), or a manner of death considered to be "fault" of the deceased (AIDS, suicide, drug overdose, etc.), or the simple fact that the deceased was not the legal spouse of the person left behind…

The description continues:

Because of the lack of social recognition, disenfranchised grief is a hidden grief and this "hiddenness" can paradoxically increase the reaction to loss...It can intensify feelings of anger, guilt and/or powerlessness, thus resulting in a more complicated grief response. Rituals may be absent or the grievers may be excluded from rituals...

Disenfranchised grief may lay hidden for years, only to be triggered by later losses...

That about covers it, doesn't it? There were all manner of bereavement support groups around at that time, but none, as far as I know, were for AIDS Caseworkers Who Fell in Love With Their Drug-Addict Clients. There wouldn't even be a good acronym that you could make up for that.

The blog posts quickly began to become melancholy and introspective, rather than just simple accounts of the "facts" as I remembered them at that point. Some time in September, I posted this:

It's hard, reliving this. I've done it two or three times over the past 16 years, and written about it in bits and pieces, but this time I've promised myself that I would get it all down, leaving nothing out, especially the parts that force me to confront all the ways in which I was wrong, selfish, confused, deluded, cruel.

These past few days they've all come close again—David, my grandmother, Sammy, the man in the white robes, all the people I met in their homes, their crummy hotel rooms, the hospitals, sitting among their cans of Sustecal, their teddy bears, their pill bottles, their memories of who they were before they got sick. But David especially. It's as if he's been standing just behind me in that quiet, polite way of his, and passing over my dreams like a gauzy veil. It's not an unpleasant feeling.

I've missed him intermittently over the years, once the initial immediacy of the loss had finally passed. I miss him now, and I just made it worse by listening to Bruce Springsteen's "Streets of Philadelphia," which I've never been able to hear without

143

crying. I don't understand how Springsteen knew how to write that song—he might have taken the words straight from David's mind toward the end, before his mind was lost altogether:

> *"...Ain't no angel gonna greet me;*
> *It's just you and I, my friend.*
> *And my clothes don't fit me no more...*
> *...Night is falling and I'm lying awake;*
> *I can feel myself fading away..."*

I don't feel like talking to anyone right now, just as I didn't feel like it then, in the spring of 1990. But I'll have to—just as I had to then. I have a family now. David told me I would, when I couldn't possibly have imagined it myself.

Mexico

By October of 2006, working on the blog about David had begun to make feel that I would lose my mind if I never had a chance to speak to him somehow, to believe that I could tell him the things I'd never had a chance to tell him, and know that he could hear me. I wrote:

Yesterday someone emailed me to ask me if I could take care of a bird she'd found. The bird had flown into the glass of a closed window, and was just sitting on the sidewalk, dazed and bleeding.

I think I understand how a bird feels, flying against glass, thinking that there's something beyond it that he needs and not understanding why he can't get to it, forgetting over and over that it's impossible, that he'll never get in. I felt that way just after David died, and I feel that way now. I keep thinking that I can get to him, if I just try hard enough.

Around that same time, I was sent to Mexico for a magazine assignment. By coincidence, I arrived on October 31st, the first of the Days of the Dead. On my second day there, I posted:

The people here create altars for their dead on these days, setting out candles, images of saints, photographs of those who have died, cigarettes, tequila, sweets, the things the things they loved when they were alive. It's believed that the souls of the dead return and partake of the essence of the food and drink left out for them, leaving what's left for the living. Yesterday someone gave me a book about Hanal Pixan, *the Mayan ritual of the dead, and I found this passage*:

"...it is also common to set up an altar to the solitary soul, dedicated to all those deceased who have no one to remember them on Earth, or who have no known relatives, or relatives who showed no interest in them.

145

It might also be...the sick who were abandoned by their relatives..."

Well, my solitary soul, I'll need to set up your altar here, in a room at the Ritz-Carlton in Cancun, overlooking the sea. There are bottles of water here, a bowl of fruit, a red flower, and a warm breeze from the sea blowing the curtains around. If you come back, I'll be waiting here, in a place nothing like the one you left—the kind of place we used to talk about visiting together.

These past few weeks, I've been willing to believe in almost anything.

The following day I wrote:

"I don't know who I am any more."

David said this to me at some point, when everything that he said, when he could speak at all, seemed to have drifted up from the bottom of a sea inside of him, carrying bits of debris accumulated over his 42 years, all the sad ideas about the past and acknowledgment of what was about to happen to him, from behind the haunted eyes that were beginning to see things that no one else could see.

I'm not sure of who I am just now, feeling his loss now again as sharply as I did then, listening to "Streets of Philadelphia" again and again, straddling the fence between the worlds of the living and the dead, and leaning toward the latter. I'm 45, alone now in an elegant room on the beach in Mexico overlooking the sea, and I don't really care about anything except just having a few moments more to understand some things, to apologize, to finally get that kiss, and let him go again. I've been hoping for dreams about him; yesterday morning I woke up very early and said a silent kind of prayer to have one, and when I slept again I had a momentary one: following him down a jetway toward a plane, watching his back as he walked onto the plane, waking up again before I could go with him.

I looked forward to coming here to Mexico, to having four nights to be alone, in a sense, with David, to having the privacy

146

to figure out what the hell has been happening to me since I started writing this, and what I'm supposed to do about it.

We used to talk about leaving New York to live near the beach, or in the country somewhere, as if we were two ordinary people who expected to have a long life together, making ordinary decisions about where we should live it. We got so lost in hope and fantasy sometimes that we even talked about somehow having a child. For as long as we could, we lived like children ourselves, playing house, pretending. When David went into the hospital, we no longer had the seclusion we needed to keep the fantasies going. It was startling to find ourselves caught between the shallow, hard fluorescent lights and cold floors of those identical hospital rooms and hallways, among people who just lived, and who saw nothing special about either of us.

I would give anything to have had a chance to bring him here, to see him eat good food, sleep on a soft mattress among white cotton sheets in a spotless room overlooking the sea, take a bath in a clean bathtub in privacy, and, afterwards, put on a thick terry robe and spend the afternoon watching the waves coming in and the sun slowly going down.

We should have gone somewhere when we had the chance. I wonder why we didn't—it wasn't as if reality held sway over us, at least in the beginning.

On my final morning in Mexico, I wrote:

Yesterday the anger came back. It was something that I remembered very well from sixteen years ago. I was sitting in the restaurant at the Ritz-Carlton, with a view to the pool. They disgusted me, all the innocent tourists asking for more coffee, discussing meetings, striding across the perfect landscape toward the pool in their new swimsuits with nothing on their minds but pleasure. If any of them saw David there, hunched and peeling, with swollen feet and an abscess on his neck, in his cheap clothes, what would they have done?

For all I knew, they were kind, compassionate people. It was only the force of my anger that prevented me from thinking that that was not the case. I despised them all.

147

Cold

In November of 2006 I posted this on my blog:

It's cold today, colder than it's been since the end of summer—the windy, bright, hard kind of cold that whips away at you until you're exhausted from it, the kind that makes you feel that you'll never be warm again.

The cold made me think about David's clothes, and his jacket in particular. The outside of it was that cheap brown vinyl that's meant to look like leather, but that seems to draw the cold right down into the flesh instead of insulating against it; it was old, and cracked and broken in places, and the quilted lining on the inside had holes through which some flimsy polyester filling showed. He had to go so many places in the cold, in that crummy jacket.

He didn't have many clothes left at all. I always imagine him either in the jacket, a pair of jeans, a plaid flannel shirt, and boots, or, at home, in the white thermal shirt and long johns I bought him. I guess I bought him the boots too, and a scarf. I still have the jacket and the plaid shirt, and maybe the boots, out at the house in Long Island where I buried his ashes. After he died I used to hold the shirt to my face to smell him in it, as people do when they're mourning, and willing to do anything to remember. And I wore the thermal shirt, stained from where the abscess broke, for a long time, too.

(Here I should say that I'm listening once again to "Streets of Philadelphia" as I write this. It's not just the lyrics that bring me to tears; Springsteen's voice in the song is also like David's—soft, a little raspy like heroin addicts' voices tend to be, with a bit of a Midwestern flatness. Springsteen even managed to look like David in the video he made for the song, with his slightly stooped, wiry body, his goatee and mustache, his tousled hair, the hooded jacket under the other one, the way he grits his teeth a little as he sings. There's even a part at the beginning where he turns, stiffly, almost as if it hurts him, to

148

look back for a moment—exactly as David would have done it. The eyes, though, are different; David's were more haunted, more beautiful.)

David was always cold that winter, unless he had a fever, or night sweats. Some nights he'd tremble with chills for a long time before going to sleep, and I'd try to warm him by sleeping with my back flat against his, or curling up around his body, my own body touching his as much as I could manage. I got into the habit of putting my palm to his forehead to check for fever, taking the opportunity to gently brush his hair back with my hand. I do that with my son now sometimes, when he's sick.

I thought a lot about the fact that there had been a point at which an AIDS diagnosis went rather suddenly (it seemed to me, in retrospect) from being a death sentence that would be carried out with fierce and merciless efficiency within a year, or maybe two, to something that might allow for indefinite survival. It seemed to me that, had David been infected a year or two later, or if he'd somehow managed to live another year or so, that he might still be alive, or at least that we might have had more than eight months together. In my blog I wrote:

I just read an article that said that Americans with HIV now have about a 24-year life expectancy. I'm glad; I don't know if any of us, back in 1989, would have believed that something like that might be possible.

I'm glad, but it also breaks my heart.

David, Springsteen, Charlie Chaplin, and God

My son, who has never been one to miss much, was eight when I started to go into my free-fall of grief. He couldn't help but notice, and I told him about David and tried to explain. In a blog post that fall or winter, I wrote:

I was just watching the "Streets of Philadelphia" video again, and again being startled by how much Springsteen resembles David, at least in the video. It's in his face, mannerisms, clothes—everything right down to how he starts to turn his head as if to look behind him toward the beginning, but stops, as if it might hurt to turn more. Sometimes I've thought I was imagining it, that I was letting myself get carried away.

But while I was watching this time, my son (to whom I've shown pictures of David, so that he'd have an idea of what the man whose ashes are buried in the yard at his grandmother's house looked like) walked over and watched it with me. "Is that David?" he asked.

So now I can say that, at least on that one point, I'm not delusional. Not completely. Springsteen, however, might see it differently.

Another post read:

I've been kind of a wreck, writing this. Last night my son and I were watching Charlie Chaplin's City Lights, *and I (for the third time that day) started to cry during the last scene. My son asked me why I was crying, and I told him that writing about my friend was making me miss him.*

"I bet he's in Heaven, asking God for some popcorn so he can watch the movie of you," my son said.

It's nice to imagine that. I love my son. He really wants to believe in Heaven.

Impractical Mind

I struggled with a way to think about my eight months with David; my feelings were mercurial:

If he hadn't been dying, if I hadn't been adrift in dreams of whatever it was I thought I should be at the time, if someone else had been handed his case file on that rainy August afternoon, it never would have happened. And if, by chance, he had lived, it never would have worked for long—he would have continued to be an addict, and I would have become one too, or found some other fantasy. I know these things. Circumstances are everything, and nothing. But things went as they did, and that makes them no less significant, or less real, or less difficult to reconcile, to make amends for, now. With one more day, and a little wisdom, I might have been able to make it all into something I could have lived with for the rest of my life.

On the other hand, maybe in saying that it wouldn't have worked out I'm just doing what I've tended to do regarding anything about David for too long—anticipating being thought foolish, a dreamer, afflicted with an impractical mind, and fending off scorn and disapproval. Who's to say that it couldn't have lasted, and been something good?

Then, a short time later:

My best dreams have always been about letting go, giving in, doing what common sense and other people would caution against—my dream about the kiss, for example. My best dreams are the dreams of an impractical mind.

More and more, I gave my "impractical mind" free rein:

As tempting as it might have been at various times in my life, and in spite of a strange incident shortly after my father's suicide when I was five or six for which I've never found a suitable explanation, I've never believed much in ghosts. My impractical mind is usually not quite impractical enough to think that the notion of ghosts, spirits, Heaven, reincarnation, etc., are not simply the results of the perfectly natural, desperate human need to not believe that after death there is absolutely nothing.

Two or three nights ago, however, I was in bed, listening to music, thinking about David, crying again. After a while the crying stopped, and I turned the music off and lay on my back waiting for sleep, hoping to dream. I felt, for just half a moment, a breezed on my left cheek—like the breath of an infant, but cool. There was nothing else but that. I opened my eyes, wondering what it was. And then my impractical mind whispered to me, Maybe it was him.

As I said earlier, I'm willing to believe almost anything these days.

Thanksgiving

On the day after Thanksgiving, 2006, I posted an entry on my blog that began as a description of how David and I had spent the various holidays of our eight months together. By that time I was in full emotional free-fall. I could barely eat, or speak. (The process was making me physically ill as well; it was around that time that I started to have bouts of gastrointestinal problems, the pain of which made me moan and yell all night sometimes, and was enough to send me to the emergency room on two occasions.) I would spend every evening chain-smoking, drinking wine, and listening to songs that reminded me of David on my iPod (I'd keep listening after I'd gone to bed, too, so that my tears rolled out from the sides of my eyes and into the ear buds in my ears). Obsessively, night and day, I went over in my mind what I would tell David if I had the chance—how much I'd loved him, how sorry I was for the ways in which I'd failed him, how much I regretted not having accepted his kiss that fall or winter day nearly seventeen years earlier. It was as if I'd just lost him, and yet even more unbearable than it had been the first time around. I wrote:

There is no resolution. I feel as if I've been diving for weeks, holding my breath until everything around me starts to fade and go dark, looking for something that isn't there any more, coming up with nothing, diving again. There's no revelation that I will have, no neat ending, no miraculous insight except that there will be no miraculous insight. I loved someone about whom I knew almost nothing, and I left him when I should have stayed, and buried him without a marker, and let myself forget for years, even though I'm the only one left who could, or would, bother to remember. I've reached the end of the story without being able to explain what it was about him that made me love him, that made him more than someone whom most people would cross the street to avoid. And what difference would it make, even if I had?

My husband, who had been reading the blog and realizing that his suspicions about my feelings for David were not only absolutely correct, but also that those feelings were utterly unresolved, was furious with me, but it was impossible for me to keep any of it hidden away inside any more, or close the floodgates once they'd been opened. I kept myself together as well as I could when my son, who was eight at the time, was around; beyond that, I was useless.

But the end of the Thanksgiving post describes what I didn't realize until a little later was a turning point, the beginning of the part of the journey that would save me from drowning.

The post read:

Of course I thought about that Thanksgiving, seventeen years ago, yesterday. At the end of the day, I looked out from my bed through the window, through the cold rain and bare, swaying trees, and toward the sky, like a child saying her prayers, believing that Heaven, and God, and Santa Claus, are always up above. I made a wish, or a prayer, a request that, as far as I was concerned, could be interpreted in any way by anyone capable of granting it, as long as it would be granted. I made my wish deliberately vague and open to interpretation so as to give it its best chance. I asked for a day, or an hour, or a few minutes, or—failing everything else—a dream. An opportunity, a little time to have one more chance to do what I needed to do and say what I needed to say to make things right with David.

All night I dreamed, and I kept waking up to take stock of what I had dreamed and remember whether or not it had been about David, but it was always something else. Finally,

154

toward morning, I had it: I met David in an airport or some kind of station, and we got on a bus. He sat next to the window. I had my hand on his knee, over his old jeans, and my head on his shoulder. He was thin; this was David in his last few weeks. There were people in the seats next to us across the aisle, and they kept talking to me, keeping me from saying what I needed to say to David.

When I woke up I wondered if that counted, or if I could ask for another chance. Like a child.

A few weeks later, I learned that someone definitely listens when I pray, but answers in unexpected ways.

Steve

My renewed and nearly disabling grief had also made me feel that, given the unlikelihood that I would get to speak to David again, I had to at least know more about his life before I met him. I was desperate to figure out a way to get in touch with someone in his family, although I'd completely lost touch with them shortly after David died, and had no idea where they might be.

The day after Thanksgiving, after making the post to my blog about the dream and the prayer, on a sudden hunch that seemed to come from nowhere, I found out what had happened to David's half-brother, Steve, who had been seven years younger than David, and who I'd met for a few minutes in the hospital on the day David died.

He'd died in 1993, at the age of 39. I found out by doing a search on the Kansas Department of Corrections website; I was surprised to see how much information I was able to get by simply filling in his name and approximate age. The record went all the way back to 1981, and listed his convictions—forgery, bad checks--nothing violent. There was no indication there of how he died, but from there I found an archived newspaper article describing his sad and violent death. From what he'd told me about himself when he wrote me a letter from prison in June, shortly after David died, it was pretty much an inevitability that things would not end well for him. Part of the letter read:

I loved David and miss him but I know he is finally out of the misery of ripping and running and the day to day existence of a drug addict. I like being alive but I can't help but sometimes wish I was with him and the struggle was over.

The letter was neat, well written, articulate, and very sad. I'd hoped that it would tell me more about David, but it was more about Steve than anything else; it was a confession to someone whose face he'd never have to look into again. This is what he did say about David:

I'm really glad that David had someone as special as you, so close to him at the end. He really had a hard life and never felt settled down inside himself.

At the time, I wrote him a long letter in reply, but it was returned to me. When I found it again recently, it brought back a few of the memories I'd lost about David and how I'd spent my time after he died, and of how frustrated and conflicted it made me feel to know that I'd in all likelihood never know how much of what David had told me about his life before I met him was actually true. It also gave me proof that time hadn't whitewashed my feelings about the kind of person he was, at least during his time with me. Perhaps, like Steve, I was confessing to a person whose face I'd probably never see again, and I may have been more honest in my letter to him than I was with anyone else. Part of it read:

For some reason I've spent most of my time lately being either "nervous as a cat" (to use David's expression) or exhausted, and I've been unable to do much more than concentrate on not climbing out of my skin or not falling asleep. It's taking a long time for me to get used to coming home every night instead of spending almost all my time at David's. Every so often I still have to say to myself, "Oh. He's not coming back." Sometimes it makes me angry; usually I'm just surprised or sad...

When I'm writing to you or your mother I'm tempted to say, "Tell me the Story of David's Life, Part I, from start to finish, and don't leave anything out." But I still don't know if I could stand hearing it, and I know it's the wrong thing to do. I don't even know why it should matter to me now, except that I love David and I wonder what happened in his life to make him the way he was. He was probably the most gentle man I ever met, which you might be giggling about right now because I'm sure (he told me) that David had some pretty violent episodes in his life...

Your letter really got me thinking about what it must be like to be addicted to heroin. People like to romanticize it sometimes—I guess I've been guilty of that too. I've tried a lot of things but always stopped short of getting into trouble for some reason. David told me that he was twelve the first time he got high, and he tried to explain a few times what it was like to care about nothing else but finding more dope. But he really wasn't like any of the other junkies I've ever met. He did think about other things, unlike most of his friends from the methadone program, and there were a lot of other things he wanted to do....It sounds strange, but in a way I think that having AIDS gave David a reason to stop getting high, and that was fine with him. It didn't seem important to him when I knew him...It must have been hard for him, finding out that he was dying and at the same time dealing with being straight for the first time in thirty years...

When I think of the man David could be now if he'd been able to stop earlier it seems like an unbelievable waste. That doesn't mean that I didn't respect him for who he was anyway, but I can't tell you how much I wish I'd met him years ago and somehow stopped him from having to die like he did (I probably couldn't have). He changed my life enormously...

I wonder if I was being disingenuous, fooling myself, by letting myself think that searching for the truth about David's life—a truth so expertly buried beneath the web of stories that David told that by the time he died perhaps even he wasn't sure any more what was true, and what wasn't—would be a betrayal. It's taken a very long time to see that, in all likelihood, that's what he wanted me to do, and it's one of the reasons he asked me to write a book about him. The truth, which came out in bits and pieces as I spoke to his sister, his daughters, and others, was not always easy to hear, and yet once I mentally put everything in context, and also looked at it in terms of the way David acted and treated me when he was no longer completely at the mercy of his addiction, I understood it, and I understood that the lies he told were for the most part tales from the life of the man he really wanted to be. Learning the truth about David wasn't a betrayal at all. What I'd really been afraid of, I think, was finding out that he really wasn't the man I thought he was at all. But he was.

Part of that fear was also that I would somehow be forced to realize that loving a man who had lived the kind of life that David had meant only that there was something wrong with me—some flaw in my personal system of morality, something simply lacking in my understanding of the world and of myself. In the letter to Steve I also wrote:

Today I'm especially nervous (I hope I don't sound completely neurotic). Yesterday I had a big discussion with my coworkers about "addictophobia", which means, obviously, fear of addicts. I don't understand how so many people who work with people who have AIDS really dislike and mistrust addicts. I was trying to explain to them (as politely as I could, but it wasn't easy) that just because a person is addicted to drugs doesn't make him or her a bad person, and that we weren't helping anyone by treating them like another species. I probably have a lot of prejudices, but that's not one of them. I don't know if I got through to anyone. Damn I have a weird job.

My nervousness, if I remember enough about who I was at that time to guess, was a result of my tendency, at least at that point, to second-guess myself, and to believe that even when I felt something very strongly about something it was likely that others' opinions

159

ultimately held more weight. I was, again, afraid that I might be wrong in my belief that addiction wasn't an indication that a person was intrinsically bad, and that by being respectful and compassionate to the addicts we worked with we might give them what they needed to change their lives, or at least give them a little peace. Maybe I really was, as I was told over and over, just being naïve, and being an "enabler".

But I've grown up enough to see that my beliefs are as valid as anyone else's (and perhaps based more on experience than those of many others who make judgments about the character of addicts and people who live on the street), and aren't negated by someone else's disagreeing with them. Almost all of us are, to a greater or lesser degree, addicted to something. We all lie, often without even thinking of it as lying. We all manipulate others in order to get what we want, and we've all stolen or cheated in one way or another—even those of us who have everything we need already. We've all caused others emotional or physical pain. And if being an "enabler", with David or with anyone else in a similar position, meant that I was giving them the comfort of feeling that they were, after all, as worthy of love as anyone else, I had nothing to be ashamed of. I only wish that I'd been secure enough to prevent that knowledge from being, if only in subtle ways that may have affected the way I dealt with David sometimes, undermined by what others told me.

Steve had pointed out in the letter that all of his siblings had different last names, but I didn't remember the others' names any more. All I wanted to do was find someone who could tell me what I never found out on my own about David, and Steve had been the only one I knew who could do that. I was determined to try, but I didn't think that I'd ever be able to find anyone else in that strange, sad family.

Deedee

I don't know what, if anything, I expected to happen when I made my little prayer, or wish, or whatever it was, looking up through the wet branches from my bedroom window, on Thanksgiving night.

What did happen shortly after was not, at any rate, something that I ever imagined could happen at that point; it was something that I'd pretty much given up hoping for. Short of waking up in the morning to find that it was November of 1989 again, and seeing David still sleeping next to me, it was the closest thing to a miracle that I could have wished for.

Along with David's half-brother's prison record and the article about the circumstances of his death, I was also able to find his obituary online in some newspaper archives a few days later. It mentioned where David's sisters were living at the time of his death. I figured that it was pretty unlikely that, thirteen years later, they would still be there, but I looked for their phone numbers. I found one.

About an hour later I was talking to David's younger sister, Deedee, who was one of the few people from his past that I could remember hearing him speak about with any real affection. At first, I babbled like an idiot, nervous that she wouldn't remember me, or that she wouldn't want to hear from me, and not even sure what I needed to say to her, and to hear.

But she did remember me, and it felt almost as if she'd been expecting me to call; she seemed to know what I needed before I did, as David often had. It's hard to describe what it felt like, talking to David's sister after all those years. Suddenly there was someone else on earth, alive and accessible and warm, connected to him by blood, who knew him well, and who had loved him as much as I did. No—it's easy to describe: I didn't feel so lonely anymore, and it was easier to breathe.

We talked for a while, and she promised to email me the next day and begin to tell me who David was before I met him, what was true and what wasn't, what his life had been like. That night, I sent her what I'd written so far about my life with David, so that there wouldn't be any question in her mind about what he'd meant to me.

The next day, as promised, she started writing to me, and telling me about David's life.

Little Things

Details had started coming back to me of their own accord. One of my blog posts from that time read:

It's still hard to understand how there can be so much that I don't remember, or that it turns out I remember altogether differently from the way things actually happened—big things—what he told me about his children (selfishly, I'd pretty much let myself forget altogether that he'd mentioned them at all, until his sister reminded me years later of their existence, and I remembered that he'd talked about them all the time), how we began to talk about his death—and yet there are so many small details that I can see or feel with such absolute clarity in my mind that when I remember them they might actually be happening again.

I remember how stiff and cold and wrinkled his jacket felt where it bent at the inside of his elbow when I took his arm as we walked outside in the winter. I remember how thin, how insubstantial against the onslaught of infections, his body felt under the waffled white long johns that he wore to bed at night, his shoulder blades like the bones inside bird wings. I know that I sometimes put my head on his chest when we were just lying around at home, talking or watching television, because when I imagine myself doing it now I immediately feel an old instinct to hold back, to do it as gently as possible so as not to hurt him. I can even see myself in the kitchen, dipping shrimp one at a time into a bowlful of batter under the warm yellow kitchen light while he waited, sitting in half-darkness on the bed. I remember that our sheets were navy blue, and that the comforter was a strange crosshatch of yellow, pinks, blues, and whites. I remember at just what point the icy smoothness of his forehead met the soft curls of his hair when my hand made the slow journey from his brow upward, searching for fever or wiping away the dampness after the fever had broken. I remember how cool and soft and loose over the bone the skin on his arm felt when I rested my hand on it the day before he died. In a room crowded with men, I would still be able to pick out his voice, and his laugh.

Truth

As she'd promised to do, David's sister, Deedee, quickly wrote back to me after reading what I'd sent her of what I'd already written about my time with her brother, and began to tell me about David's life.

I was ashamed, and I still am, that there was so much that David had told me about during our long days and nights together that I'd forgotten about, or, worse, had simply discounted, knowing his propensity to make things up. (No doubt some of the "You can't believe anything a junkie tells you" position that many people in the field—and even a lot of drug users themselves—took had an effect as well, even though, as I said, I did try to keep an open mind about the things my clients told me.) In my own defense, perhaps I can say that my obsessive preoccupation with trying to keep him with me for as long as possible obscured anything not associated with that, but it's a lame excuse. Clearly, it had been very important to him that his life be remembered by someone who cared, and recorded so that he could at least die without feeling that his existence on earth would not seem inconsequential, or a complete waste. That, I believe, is one of the reasons he asked me to write his book.

The more I read of what Deedee told me, the more I remembered of some of the things he'd told me, and I realized that he'd actually told me the truth about much of his life, but had often downplayed the pain of the abuse and neglect he'd been subjected to as a child. His drug use, of course, was enough of a testament to that.

As I said, one thing that I did know about David from the first day I met him was how important it was to him that he had Chippewa blood. He would often tell me about the time he'd spent on "the rez" in Minnesota—so much so, it seems, that I had it in my head that he had spent most of his life there, although that was not the case.

I had met David's biological mother, Frances (a woman toward whom, for reasons that would soon become clear, David had no great affection), in the hospital about an hour after he died, and I remember how adamant she'd been that David did not, in fact, have Indian blood. "He was always playing Indian," she'd told me. "But he wasn't Indian." It confused me; I didn't understand at the time (knowing as I did so little about the world beyond my own tiny one) why she would deny it if it were true, and I wondered if David had made the story up. At the time, I was in no shape to try to sort things out.

But Deedee, who had read of my confusion about the subject in what I'd sent her, sorted it out for me in no uncertain terms in the first paragraph of her first email about David's life:

Just to clarify one thing to begin with...David's father WAS Indian, a fact that his mother was well acquainted with. Why she felt the need to invalidate him even at that point is beyond me. Suffice it to say that she was a self-absorbed, hyper-critical, mean-spirited, and embittered woman.

He'd told me the truth about that. It was one of the few things that he'd been proud of. It had meant so much to him, and his mother had denied it, apparently, all his life, right up to an hour or two after his death.

Deedee, David's sister, had done a great deal of research into her own family's splintered history over the years, partly, I guess, out of curiosity, and partly out of necessity. When she was 24 (having searched for, and found, their birth mother just before she turned 21) she located their biological father, Paul. Her sister, Suzy, wasn't interested in meeting him, but Deedee and David went, on separate occasions, to visit him in Minnesota. She wrote to me:

I spent one day with him (July 3 1974, I think), then we had to leave (to go back to where) Suzy and I were living at the time. In April of the next year, he died, so I never saw him again. Was he kind? I don't have any idea. He was nice to us the day we spent with him, but he was on his best behavior. I just remember that I didn't get a critical attitude from him, and that his younger children didn't hate him, so that must mean something. But he definitely was a con-artist, and went to prison numerous times for various offenses. He had three kids before we came along, then eight more with another woman after my mother.

David's own experiences in trying to assert his Native American ancestry, it turned out, were very similar to his father's. Deedee wrote:

…our father devoted a substantial amount of time to trying to verify his Indian ancestry. Clearly, he physically looked Indian, right down to the 'cliché' red skin tone, and inability to grow much facial hair, especially side-burns. The summer before his death, however, he was sporting a very nice moustache; he was an extremely attractive man. I think I have deduced that the difficulty my father had in 'proving' his ancestry stemmed from a 'lie' written on his birth certificate—to the effect that his mother was 'white'.

That was undoubtedly put there by his father, who was not particularly in love with the fact that she, in fact, was not white. My (and David's of course) grandfather was born in Canada in 1878. He spent the first part of his life (about the first 25 yrs. or so) in Canada. Then… he and his brother decided they were going to become wilderness guys, and go to the States, and that they both were going to marry Indian women. It seems to me to have been a decision based on practical concerns. We're talking here about the first decade of the 20th century, remember. They wanted to live in the wilderness, and who else but a 'squaw' would have agreed to live that way or would have had the 'know-how'…Jesse developed the habit of 'renting out' his 'wife' to the men in the logging camps to make himself some fast cash, and then denying paternity when she became pregnant. He sounds like pretty much of a self-serving snake. After he was done with her, he sent her on her way, but not before taking her kids from her and putting them in foster homes, where, I understand, our father grew up. She probably went back to the rez where she later died…After dumping his Indian wife, Jesse married a proper white woman and lived a 'decent' life… Jesse was undoubtedly ashamed of the fact that his first wife was Indian, and lied on the birth certificates of their children, saying that she was white. Who knows, maybe with such prejudice around, he lied to protect his children, to obscure their Indian ancestry. But my father dealt with the effects of that lie for the remainder of his life.

In New York, there's an agency set up to provide social and other services to people of Native American ancestry. Back around the time that I knew David, they also offered various kinds of assistance to their clients who had AIDS; they may still do that. Shortly after David died, when I was trying to arrange his memorial service, I called them to ask if they might be of any help, or if they had any suggestions as to how to incorporate David's cultural heritage into the service (by that time I'd decided that I should trust David's version of the truth more than I did his mother's). When I gave the man I was speaking to David's name, he recognized it. David, he assured me, had tried to scam them; his background was not Native American. With his father dead, and his mother in denial, and any records falsified, he wouldn't have had any way to prove it, I suppose. It must have hurt him. It undoubtedly would have hurt him to know that, although something inside me

169

Drawing

Shortly after I began to correspond with David's sister, I noticed an old portfolio at the back of my closet, and pulled it out to look inside. Among my son's artwork from kindergarten, I found a pile of drawings and paintings—done in charcoal, watercolor, pastels, crayon, Japanese ink, and anything else that I had around at the time—that I had made years earlier, in the mid-90's. I'd never been able to draw worth a damn before that time, and I wouldn't be able to do it now, but some of the pictures were surprisingly beautiful; I felt as if I were looking at someone else's work. Almost all of them had been done about six years after David died, and one or two years after I married my husband. At the time, my husband and I had been living in the Peter Cooper Village apartment down the street from the V.A. Hospital and Bellevue—the one in which I used to wait for visiting hours to start, so that I could see David in the evenings after work, the one I'd lived in as a child, where I dreamed that I could fly.

One of the drawings, done in brown and black pastels, is a picture of David on the day I watched him sleeping, his clothing loosened so that he was nearly naked, in his private (because of the TB) room at the hospital. I remember drawing it—I did it completely from memory, amazed at how clearly I still saw the scene six years after his death, and how effortless it felt to put memory on paper. I don't even think I knew what I was drawing until it began to take form on the page; it wasn't something I'd planned to do. I got his face wrong; I was always particularly bad at drawing faces. But somehow I managed to capture the essence of the scene. His face, relaxed and

171

peaceful in sleep, is turned toward the window, where a pitcher with a single, slightly wilted rose has been placed, and his hair is long and pushed back from his forehead in soft, disarrayed curls, as if I'd brushed it back myself. His arm is thin; there's a hospital bracelet on his wrist that is much too loose, and his hand—perhaps only because of my lack of skill—is tiny, thin, delicate as a bird-claw, with the ring that I gave him on his middle finger. Instead of the pale afternoon light that came in from the window that day, I've drawn a night scene, all buildings with bright windows, and black sky and stars. After all those years, and after so many other things had changed in my life, I still drew every mark on that piece of paper with an anguished love that I think would be evident to anyone.

And then I remembered something that Deedee had said in one of her emails:

David was very smart, and very talented as well. He was quite an artist. Did you ever see any of his work? He drew mostly in pastels.

David had never told me that he drew. As I'd been in the weeks after David died, I was willing at that point to believe anything that would make me feel that he was close by.

The ring I'd drawn on David's finger was the second one I'd given him to replace the one he'd lost, or traded for extra methadone, or given away. It was silver, with an inlay of something like black onyx. I'd recently started to wear it again because my need to feel connected in some way with David again had become so great, and so painful.

In my blog, I'd written this about that second ring:

Why, David, was the ring off of your finger, buried in the tangle of white hospital sheets around you, when I came back to your room and found that you had, in spite of my determination that it would never happen that way, died alone?

At the time, as I had on the day David died, I felt that I might go out of my mind if I didn't find a way to understand what, if anything, that had meant.

Water

The more I think about David's life, and about my own, the more I wonder how it is that some people seem to be blessed in almost every aspect of their lives, and others seem to have been born into lives in which there are no opportunities for happiness, for love, for almost any of the elements that most people think of as the things that make life worth living. In spite of the many stupid mistakes I've made in my life, in spite of all the ways in which things could, and perhaps should, have gone wrong for me, I've always been kept safe, and been given what I needed, and much more, without even having to ask.

David, on the other hand, had been born directly into hell, his life ruined almost before it started. In his sister Deedee's words, he never had a chance.

Deedee, when I finally got in touch with her, confirmed some of the things that David had told me, in a remarkably calm and innocuous (so much so that I had forgotten much of it until I was reminded years later) way, when he was alive, and filled me in with nothing held back on what he either hadn't told me, or I'd forgotten, on the horror of their childhoods—David's in particular.

David was born in Michigan in 1947. Besides Deedee, who was the youngest of his siblings, David also had a sister named Suzy, who was born just under a year after he was, and an older brother whose name was Michael. When David was about three, and his sisters roughly one and two, his father went to prison, and their mother put them into a Catholic orphanage in Minnesota. A year or so later, having met a new man, their mother took her children back "out of the pawn shop," as Deedee put it.

A very short time after the children went back to live with their mother, Michael drowned. It was one of the incidents from David's life about which he'd told me but which, inexplicably, I'd forgotten until Deedee reminded me.

During that time, I was still obsessively going through everything I'd ever written about David. Every time I thought I'd found everything there was to find, it seemed, something else would turn up. One day, after Deedee had reminded me about the drowning, among the pages of the novel I'd tried to write about David years earlier, I found this, which began with a description of "Sam" sitting alone at night in the hospital visitors' room, and ends with my fictionalized (to what extent I'm still not sure) version of the drowning as David had described it to me:

Some nights, if he could make it past the nurses' station without being seen, he'd take his cigarettes and go down to the visitors' room to sit in the dark and look down at the river and think. Across the water Queens flickered under the heavy, hot sky, and he imagined he could see where the island ended and the black Atlantic began. It scared him a little to think of all that water lurching back and forth in a basin that was unimaginably deep and wide, and of all the things alive and dead in it.

One night when he was weak and his thoughts weren't controlled he started to remember way back, to the first time he saw water that big and thought about it like that, on Lake Superior. He didn't remember getting there, and he didn't remember leaving.

He remembered layers: the strip of white between him and Frank, the narrower strip between Frank and the black line of water, the curved and moving lines of foam coming forward, the horizon neither darker nor lighter than the water but distinguishable, the gray sky and a haze at the top. Frank going in and Sam following, kicking his legs forward as he ran so that sand and then water rose high and then curved back toward him. They couldn't stop laughing. Frank made as if he was drowning, kneeing in the waves, falling back and coming up again with his arms in the air. Sam ran toward him, playing lifeguard, his voice, deepened like a man's, yelling, I'll save you. *He fell hard into a wave, hands digging into the sand, sand and water entering his eyes and mouth and nose. Coming up, he lost his bearings and found he was facing the shore again. His mother and the man were waving, and he waved back. They were running toward the water, waving, and Sam was coughing and laughing and waving, and they kept coming.*

Some time passed. He was out of the water, kneeling in the sand. Someone's hands were hard on his shoulders, pushing him deeper, arching him back. He couldn't keep the sand out of his eyes. There were people all around. His mother was crouched before him, and he was watching the thin lines crisscrossed all over her chest above her bathing suit, and smelling the sweet smell of beer and the menthol smell of the cigarettes she smoked, and she was smacking his head from side to side.

"You son of a bitch," she was saying, rhythmically, a little slurred. "You son of a bitch you drowned him son of a bitch."

Deedee hadn't told me about the exact circumstances of Michael's drowning before I found that description, and she was taken aback that I'd mentioned the beer and menthol cigarettes, as that's what David would have, in fact, smelled on his mother's breath that day. She told me what had actually happened:

It was probably within the first few days after the children were taken back out of the orphanage (it may even have been the same day) that our mother and a few of her friends arranged a picnic on the bank of a river. While the adults were getting food and beer out of the cars, the children ran on ahead down to the water. Michael, who was several years older than David,

176

went into the water, dove under, and never came back up. The men formed a kind of human chain in the water to look for him; when they found his body they saw that a little knife that Michael wore on his belt seemed to have gotten caught on some of the vegetation under the water.

I asked Deedee if it was possible that their mother had somehow made David, who was just four at the time, believe that the drowning had been his fault. I may have been somewhat off on some of the details of the description that I'd written, but it seemed that the part about his mother telling him that he had drowned Michael must have come from somewhere other than my imagination—David must have said it when he told me about the incident, or perhaps I just sensed it somehow.

Deedee, who had been only about two when the drowning occurred and had therefore heard the story, for the most part, second-hand, wrote back and said that she would certainly not have put it past their mother to transfer her feelings of guilt for not paying more attention to what the children were doing that day, and "lay it on the small shoulders of a four-year-old boy."

And that was only the beginning.

Deedee continued to write, and to tell me more about David's life as a child and a young man. Most of what she told me was incredibly difficult to read, especially when I was in so much pain already.

A few years after the children's mother got them back out of the orphanage, and Michael drowned, she put David, Deedee, and Suzy up for adoption in New Mexico—the girls to one home, and David to another couple. The two families lived a few blocks away from each other.

It was difficult enough to read that David and his sisters had been shuffled around so often, and for no apparent good reason other than their mother's convenience. In a subsequent email (in response to a question I asked her about David's time in the military), she told me about what their lives had been like after the adoptions:

Yes, David was in the service, the Army I think. I believe that he left home young in order to escape the horror that his adoptive mother inflicted upon him. I heard that she was miserable, but never, curiously, from David himself. Her name was Ellen..., the adoptive father was Richard. About a year after they adopted David, they had a daughter, whose name was Kathy...She was one of the people who told me about Ellen...She didn't say much, but here's basically the bare bones of it. Kathy was afraid that she was crazy. She was specifically afraid that she had inherited her mom's illness—and told me that she would never dare to have children of her own, for fear that she would be as wicked and cruel to them as her mom was to her and David. It was heart-wrenching to watch and listen to. No specifics were offered, but her demeanor was one of sheer terror at remembering her childhood. I know David was also horribly abused by Ellen, but again, I emphasize, not from David telling me, and it certainly couldn't *have been that he never had the opportunity. A friend from high school who happened to live in the same building as David when she was growing up told me many years later that David had been horribly abused, and had sometimes told her about specific instances. One thing she told me I have never forgotten. She said that David had told her that Ellen had discovered David masturbating once when he was a boy, and had beaten him for it—ON HIS PENIS!! Well, it's hard to imagine anything that cruel or f***** up, but I had no reason to doubt my friend, she was pretty straightforward. Another incident, the only one that I can personally testify to, happened one day (an extremely rare occurrence) when both families drove up to the mountains for a picnic together. I think I was about 8 years old, so Suzy and David were 9 and 10. I had sprained my ankle, so I couldn't go with the rest of them when they decided to take a hike on a trail. Ellen was nursing Kathy, so I had to stay behind with her, while everyone else went on the hike. No sooner had they gotten out of sight when Ellen underwent a complete transformation from a sweet, doting, pleasant mother to an absolute demonic creature. No kidding, it was horrifying to me. She turned to me and said: "Yeah, I know you, you're just like your brother aren't you? You're a black sheep just like him." Like, she had my number or something. I never told anyone about it. I doubt very seriously that I was even old enough to understand the meaning of the reference, but her demeanor left no doubt that whatever it was, it was very, very bad. Like, burn in hell bad. So I can only imagine what David and Kathy were subjected to on a daily basis…Ellen scared me out of my wits.*

I know that David had mentioned that his adoptive parents had been abusive, but if there was anger or bitterness in his accounts of what happened, it was muted—again, as if, perhaps, he'd come to believe that he'd deserved to be hurt like that. When I read Deedee's (and, later, when I met her in person, heard) much more graphic stories about what David had gone through under his adoptive parents' "care" I was filled with rage; I started to think of Richard and Ellen as indirectly responsible for David's death.

I had started to get pretty good at finding people online, and I started looking (without success, at first) for Ellen and Richard. I didn't even know if they were still alive, and I had no idea what I'd say to them if I found them. It was a month or two after Deedee first told me about them that I stumbled across their names and phone number online, and felt (as I had when I suddenly found the information about David's brother, and subsequently his sisters' whereabouts) that they'd been hidden from me until, for whatever reason, the time was right for me to find them.

Having had several glasses of wine at dinner, I dialed the number without stopping to consider what might be the proper way to approach them, or what their reaction might be, or the fact that I might not have been in a frame of mind that would prevent me from simply telling them that I hoped that they would burn in hell for what they'd done to David.

The old man, Richard, answered. He sounded a little confused, but I think I caught him off guard, before he could make the decision (as Deedee suspected he might do when I mentioned that I was looking for them) not to talk to me.

I was polite, somehow. Charming, even. Once I mentioned David, and gave the briefest of explanations as to who I was, Richard started to tell me in no uncertain terms what he'd thought of David. He was a "horrible mistake," and a "very hard child to raise," and that they'd raised him "to a point," until David "just went to pieces." Richard and his wife (who, according to David's sister, had done most of the real damage), were "sorry that they ever got involved." David ran away, stole money from his

180

teachers, and caused them, it seems, no end of trouble from the moment they brought him into their home. I was glad to hear it.

When I pointed out that David had only been eight or nine when they adopted him, and had already been put into and taken back out of an orphanage at his biological mother's convenience—hinting at the possibility that there may have been reasons for such a young child to act that way—Richard only said, "His mother—there was something wrong with her." He was also of the opinion that there was something wrong with David's sister; I told him that I had an entirely different impression of her, but that didn't seem to sink in.

Ellen, Richard told me, was sick, but when I asked him what was wrong with her, he said, "Who knows?" His response seemed to indicate the exact, and barely measurable, amount of caring or introspection to which he (and, no doubt, his wife) was able to rise.

I couldn't tell if Richard had already known that David was dead. Either way, it didn't seem to concern him much. I said something about David's having AIDS. "How'd he get that?" Richard asked, as if, after all he believed or claimed to know about David, it needed any explanation.

You'd think that he could have come up with one kind thing to say about David, who he'd known pretty much only as a child, and who had been dead for over sixteen years. One thing.

Jesus

Except for when I was a child growing up in a very Catholic family, I've never been a "religious" person in the traditional sense. I've always had a belief in God, or the Divine—the force behind the creation of everything around us—but I have stubbornly resisted, and always will, the human instinct to "put a face on God", or say with any certainty whatsoever who, or what, the Divine really is. I just have faith that he/she/they/it is there, somewhere, pulling the strings up to a point, and that he/she/they/it is a creative genius with real artistic talent and a wonderful sense of humor. And, as I said, I've always felt that I was well looked-after, for some reason.

Recently, however, I've become a big fan of Jesus—not Jesus the Son of God, not Jesus, product of the Virgin Birth, not the bloodied caricature in gaudy prints on people's walls, and certainly not the holy battering-ram used by those who chatter on about their personal relationships with him while at the same time using his image to justify the self-righteous, intolerant, and breathtakingly cruel behavior that he tried so hard to get people to change—but Jesus the man, the teacher.

Growing up, in church and Sunday school and elsewhere, I'd heard phrases like "God is love," and "Love thy neighbor as thyself,", and "Judge not, lest ye be judged," and "Blessed are the merciful," so often, and from so many hypocrites, that the words, and the things that Jesus actually tried to teach, became nothing more than empty slogans that I no longer even heard.

But I've begun to hear them again, and to understand what Jesus, the man, so desperately and ultimately in such futility tried to teach. A short time ago I was having a discussion with a man who had made a comment to the effect that the homeless should just help themselves. Thinking of David, and of all the other people I'd met and worked with over the years who had found themselves desperate and with nothing left that would be considered valuable in this world, I tried to tell the man that, once someone reaches that state of having nothing, it becomes almost impossible for him to help himself. Those people—the despised, the sick, the ones driven by circumstances to desperate acts—are the ones with whom Jesus would have wanted to spend his time, and are the ones to whom he felt God's love should be channeled through those who have the means to do so. It's those who have the advantages of wealth, education, health, and decent childhoods in which love was freely given, and who nevertheless refuse to help those without those advantages and think of them as inferior and unworthy, whom Jesus would, perhaps, despise, if he ever despised anyone.

People have sometimes told me that I had "compassion" for David. I tell them that compassion had nothing to do with it—I loved him, loved spending time with him, couldn't imagine how I could go on living my life once he was gone. I wanted to make him happy, and give him all of the things he'd never been given before, because I loved him. There was no hardship involved on my part beyond the pain of helplessly watching his life ebb away; I never thought, "I really don't feel like doing this, but I should try to be kind and compassionate to this poor man anyway." For me, the choices were easy.

And I take no credit for David's decision to "get rid of the bad things in his personality," either. For whatever reason, he came to that on his own and, as

Snow Globes

As I wrote the blog, the feelings I'd felt compelled to bury even deeper than any of the others manifested themselves in my consciousness again, insistent and refusing, finally, to be sublimated. The problem, of course, was that by then it was sixteen years and more too late; there was no outlet, no second chance—no David. It was one more unbearable regret among so many others that I didn't see how I might survive. And, as before, it seemed that there was no one who could possibly understand it, or tell me how to keep from drowning.

One of my posts described that aspect of things:

In almost every dream I've ever had about David—the one about the kiss, the one in which I'm trying to talk to him on the bus, the one about making love in the amphitheater when I was supposed to be getting married to someone else, and another recent one in which we started to make love but realized that we were in my mother's apartment, and had no privacy, there is always an interruption, something that keeps us from doing, or saying, what would be easy for most people to do or say. Sometimes it's just simply a matter of my waking up too soon. I've thought about that; it seems to reflect the way that we had to live our lives when David was alive. All of the things that we should have been able to do without thinking much of the consequences, or without having to worry what would happen if anyone else found out, like the ordinary people that we really were, had to be sublimated, postponed, left unsaid. Even in anticipation of David's most private moment, when he should have been allowed to die quietly, and only in the presence of someone who loved him, we were at the mercy of what others thought about how things should be done. It makes me so angry now, and leaves me feeling as helpless as I did back then.

There was also a second post about it that was more to the point:

My head, these days, seems to be filled with dozens of snow globes, each holding a scene from my months with David. I keep taking them out, looking at them from all angles, shaking them to see the snow fall around them once again. One of them holds the moment when David turned my face toward his, but I've changed that scene so that I accept his kiss, letting myself forget about the consequences of what will happen next, allowing it to happen. I look at it more than any of the others, turning it around and around to find the angle at which it seems the most real. Sometimes I can make it so real that I lose my breath for a moment, so real that I can barely stand it.

Wives and Daughters

There are many fragments of what I wrote at that time—stained pieces of wrinkled, cheap onion-skin typing paper, or handwritten words on lined pieces of torn-out notebook paper, from those first few weeks after David died. As I wrote the blog I gradually found more and more of them, and bits of forgotten memories would bloom into pictures that I could see in my head like latent images brought quickly into view in a bath of developer. There are also accounts of events, or of my feelings at the time, that seem to have been written by someone else; hard as I try, I don't remember them. I cried as I found things that clearly indicated that there were things that David had told me about but that, over the years, I'd forgotten, so that when Deedee told me about them I thought at first that I'd never heard them before.

I loved David. In spite of the mistakes I made at the time, and my own immaturity and self-centeredness, I thought of nothing but his happiness and health during those eight months that we had together. Clearly he had wanted, finally, to be able to tell someone who cared everything about his life and how he'd become the person he'd become. And somehow I managed to forget some of the most important pieces, like the fact that he spoke, often, of his children. I can only try the excuse that my energies were so directed toward the day-to-day tasks of trying to keep him comfortable and well that I could hardly register much else. It may also have been that I wasn't sure whether or not to believe some of the things he told me, but now I know that, although he told lies or half-truths about some of the details (perhaps no longer even always aware that he

187

was doing it), he told me the truth about the most important things, because he wanted me to know, and perhaps someday let his children know. I'm afraid that the most shameful reason—especially with regard to the existence of his children, and others who may have wanted to see him before he died—might be that I wanted him to myself, couldn't bear the thought of being pushed aside by his real family at the end, or of having to share him. I hope I'm wrong, and that David simply gave me good reason to believe that they would have no interest in seeing him. Whatever the reason, it came like a punch to the chest when Deedee reminded me about them.

David had three daughters. The first girl was nearly an adult by the time I met David, and the other two were about ten and eleven. Deedee had lost track of the oldest daughter and her mother, but she told me that she'd seen the daughter when she was about sixteen, and that she was beautiful, and looked a lot like David.

On a Sunday afternoon in the early spring of 2007, several months after I'd first gotten in touch with Deedee, while I was alone in my house and glad of the privacy, an email came in whose subject line was, "Contact from David E.'s daughter." It simply didn't register for a moment. I knew, by then, that David had had children, but to gradually grasp that I was about to read a message from the daughter of the man I'd loved so much, and lost, so long ago, stunned me as much as it would to come downstairs one morning and find him sitting on my couch (and don't think for a moment that I hadn't imagined what I would do if that happened). Even gladder of my privacy at that point, I sat looking at the subject line for a moment, and then put my face in my hands and whispered, "OK. Your daughter. OK." And then I opened it.

It started like this:

Hello.

I just got a phone-call from David E.'s sister...who told me not only had he passed in 1990, but that you took care of him for the last 8 months of his life. I'm his daughter from his first marriage...My name is Christine...

We weren't close, Dave and I. I think I saw him twice, maybe three times my entire life.

It's strange to hear so many years later that he's dead. We were all under the impression he had stayed with his second family and had finally found what he was looking for in life. So surprising to hear he was back in the city for the last leg of his journey.

I wanted to thank you for taking care of him, it's good to know that he was with someone he cared for and that cared for him in the end.

After reading the message several times, and pulling myself together, I wrote back to her, and told her that, although it was a shock, after all these years, to hear from her, I was very happy that she'd contacted me. I told her that I was sorry that she'd never had a relationship with her father, and that I believed that, had his upbringing been different, things might not have happened that way. She responded:

I've been in upstate NY since 1986. Had I known he was around and ill, I would have come to see him...I never held a grudge against my father. He did the best thing he could when he realized he wasn't into being a father or husband at the time: he moved on... Everyone travels a different road. He had one that took him in a different direction and that's okay... I look a lot like my mother, but my eyes are right from my dad, so dark they're near black. And everyone says I got his gift of gab.

My God. And I had been afraid that his daughters would hate him. Here was this smart, articulate

189

woman, who had just lost her mother three months earlier, who had just learned that her father, who had never really been part of her life at all, had died of AIDS seventeen years earlier, who knew nothing of me except for what Deedee had just told her over the phone, and she was thanking me for caring for him, and telling me that she had nothing against him. It was a huge relief, and it made it immediately clear that David, at the age of 21, had fathered an exceptionally compassionate, thoughtful person.

I wanted so badly to be able to tell him—*She would have come to see you, David.*

In my reply to Christine's first message, I wrote:

I really loved David, and, as ironic and sad as it is, I think that I might have been around him when he was at his best.

It was a risky thing for a near-stranger to say to an estranged daughter who had just learned of her father's long-ago death. Her response, though, was:

It's great to hear, Nancy. Love, when found, no matter where, should be cherished.

Amazing.

Pictures

As we continued to write to each other, Deedee telling me what she knew of the rest of the details of David's life before I met him, she and I became friends. It was as if I'd been thrown a life-line, and the fact that it was David's sister who was at the other end of it seemed almost as miraculous as if he'd thrown it himself.

Deedee did everything she could to satisfy what had become my obsessive hunger for every detail I could get about David's life, my desire to separate fiction from truth and trace, finally, at least some of the path that David had taken to the chair at my desk in August of 1989.

I've often wondered whether it might change some people's thinking if, every time they passed a homeless person or an addict or someone suffering from mental illness on the street they were forced to see a few photographs, or perhaps a video clip, of the person as a child. Maybe, I've thought, it would re-connect the willfully disconnected wires of understanding and recognition that lead to compassion and empathy.

Of course, I didn't need to see David's baby pictures in order to think of him as a human being worthy of love. Still, when I finally met Deedee in New Mexico, and she showed me an envelope full of them, I had to cry, and laugh. The image of him that I still had in my mind suddenly filled out into something that much more warm and real and sweet. But it was so painful to think of what he was going through even at the time during which the pictures were taken, and of what he would go through many years later as a result.

191

There he was as a little boy, standing with his sisters in a church, or leaning over to kiss Deedee as she sat in a high-chair, or grinning a huge, goofy smile and wearing thick, huge, nerdy glasses in an early school picture, or squinting in the sun in a yard with his dog, or fishing with his back turned to the camera. Perhaps in some of those earlier pictures he hadn't yet become aware that he and his sisters were not being treated as children should be, or that love was being withheld from them. He looks hopeful and happy, and that look in his eyes of asking without expecting to receive is not yet there.

There are fewer pictures of him as he got older, but there is one of him at around the age of fifteen—another school photograph—in which the glasses and goofy grin are gone, revealing a handsome young man who could have been in the process of trying out for the football team, or deciding which girl he'd like to ask to the prom. By then, I know, he was actually doing drugs, being beaten at home, getting into trouble at and outside of school, and on his way to being either given a choice between reform school and the army, or making the choice between the army and the abuse he was suffering on his own. He was probably still doing his pastel drawings by then, perhaps secretively in his room, as he probably did most things by then.

On the back of the photograph, David filled in the "From:" line with his name, but the "To:" space has been left blank, as if he didn't want to assume that anyone would actually want it.

Among the pictures that Deedee has, there is only one picture of David taken after that time. In it, he's probably about 23. His hair is fairly long, and he's in another yard by some clotheslines with a mischievous grin on his face clearly indicating that he's either just done, or is about to do, something he shouldn't. By then, he had gone into the army and had either been kicked out for fighting, or gone AWOL. He'd gone to New York, attended Woodstock, fathered a daughter, gotten married to her mother, and left when the baby was about six months old to live in Kansas, where his biological mother was living by then. He also, according to his sister, had a habit of hitchhiking down to Mexico every so often—no doubt for business reasons, but also because he loved it there.

It must have been shortly after that picture was taken that something happened about which—like many other things—David had told me, but I'd forgotten.

When David was in his 20's, he was good friends with a homicide detective in Wichita. I don't know exactly how that happened; David must have been working both sides of the fence to some extent, but Deedee tells me that the detective was genuinely fond of him. (The detective was also one of the lead investigators in the horrific case of serial killer Dennis Rader, who called himself "BTK"—for "Bind, Torture, Kill." David's transgressions at the time must have seemed, in comparison, pretty innocuous.)

The detective had been trying to solve the murder of a farmer and his wife (the wife had been killed with an ax) for about ten years. He knew who had committed the murder, apparently, but hadn't been able to collect enough evidence to charge him. But the man's "best friend" had recently disappeared, and the detective believed that he'd killed him, too. The problem was that no body had been found. The detective convinced David to share the man's jail cell as an informant and try to get him to tell him where the body was (it may have been an agreement worked out to reduce charges against David for something

193

else). It worked; David testified against the man, who was convicted of the murder and sentenced to life. But David had to be put in protective custody at a federal prison for a while.

This is how Deedee described the trial:

I was there that day. It was very strange. Only the prosecution, defense, (the detective), David, the judge and I were in the courtroom. It was very dimly lit, I think it was winter. There were two tables sitting side by side about 3 feet apart facing the Judge. I think David's team were on the left hand side and (the murderer's) on the right. I was in the gallery behind (right behind—as I believe that it was a small room). At one point David had to get up to take the stand to testify, and would pass between the two tables to get to the stand. (The murderer) had a pen in his hand and he kept pushing the end of it, you know alternately pushing out the point and retrieving it. I just remember thinking that he was going to use that damn pen to stab David as he walked between the tables.

Hearing the story from Deedee triggered a memory of sitting on the futon in the apartment on Suffolk Street, listening to David tell it himself in a particularly animated way while he fixed something to eat in the kitchen. I remembered wondering, at the time, why it seemed so important to him that I heard the story, and understood the danger he'd been put in by doing what he did. And yet I know that it was yet another thing that I didn't allow myself to quite believe, and therefore allowed to fade away in my memory. I pray he didn't notice, because it was something he was proud of.

Back to Suffolk Street

After one of many arguments with my husband (who was, quite reasonably, upset by its detailed confirmation of his original suspicions about my feelings for David) about the blog, I decided one day that it was time to go to Suffolk Street. And so, on an afternoon on which the weather was very much like it was the day that David and I took our first walk together, I did. Afterwards, I sat with a *cafe con leche* in *El Castillo de Jagua* on Rivington Street, which looked exactly the same as it did when David and I used to go there for late breakfasts on weekends, thinking about how I used to go downstairs to the bathroom to brush my hair and put on lipstick, so as to look decent for him, and pulling myself back together after seeing "our" building again for the first time in seventeen years.

Heading downtown on my way to the building, I hadn't been able remember which of the Fourteenth Street buses I was supposed to take, so I'd taken the Avenue D and wound up, after a long ride, on Houston, fairly well east of Suffolk. Someone had offered to sell me heroin as I walked west (it was a Friday, as it had been the day that David pointed out the "weekend warriors" from Wall Street, so perhaps the he thought that I was one as well).

I'd been a little afraid to turn onto Suffolk Street—afraid that the building might be gone, afraid that I'd start to cry and look like a fool. But the building was there. I'd forgotten how utterly nondescript it was, and it took me a minute to even be sure that I was looking at the right one (it's funny that I'd been thinking of it as the only building on that side of the street for so long, as it is decidedly not). George's tire-repair shop was gone, and the little yard next to it where the stone angels and headstones used to be had been turned into a community garden. I'd stood for a long time looking up through the glass in the front door, up the old marble steps whose front edges were as worn as they'd been back when David was carried out for the final time, up to the hallway that ran to David's door, dingy and fluorescent-lit as ever. I'd wanted to go in, but there was no one around, and I wasn't sure that I could handle it anyway.

On the front of the building was the same sign, advertising apartments for rent, that had been there the day we stood outside, waiting to see David's new apartment for the first time, both of us excited by the prospect of his having a place of his own.

With nothing left to do there except stand on the sidewalk and look suspicious or simply stupid (or like I was looking for drugs), I'd walked around the corner and found the bodega where we used to buy cigarettes and beer; it had not changed at all either. After that, I'd gone to the restaurant, which seemed as comforting and familiar as it always had. I imagined David sitting across the table from me, drinking his coffee and eager to prove to both of us that he could still "eat like a champ."

When I finished my *cafe con leche*, I felt strong enough to go back out and explore some more. I found the Essex Market, which David had introduced me to, and which is now quite a bit more upscale than it used to be; vendors were selling maki and chai lattes in addition to the Dominican botanicals, the hunks of meat and piles of fish, the tropical fruits and vegetables. The Market, and that part of the neighborhood in general, had always smelled of poultry and garlic, and it still does now. The odor of it all was like my own little taste of Proust's *madeleine,* taking me back to where I wanted to be more than anywhere else in the world just then.

"His" neighborhood, he called it. It's still his neighborhood, the one we knew together. Nothing much changes down there, except that people die or move away, and other people take their places.

I'd been trying to remember where David and I used to do our laundry. Just by chance, I found the place, around the corner from the Market, and for half a moment I could see the two of us through the window, passing the time on a Sunday afternoon, waiting for our clothes to dry. Back then, I'd never even minded spending the day performing mundane chores like doing laundry, or grocery shopping, or cleaning up the apartment, as long as David was there. I'd changed; I no longer needed to be entertained all the time. He'd changed, too. I don't know how long it had been since he'd been at leisure to spend the day doing the simple things that people do to pass a weekend day, free of the need to chase his next fix, but he seemed content—even, inexplicably, happy.

I decided that I needed to go to Suffolk Street one more time before going back home. I guess I was hoping that something would happen, that I'd be able to get inside and bravely take a big dose of whatever reaction it caused in me, but it seemed unlikely that I'd see anyone going in at that time of day, much less anyone who would be willing to let a stranger into a building in that neighborhood. So I stood for a few minutes more at the gate of the community garden, trying to look as if I was there for a good reason.

And then someone went in. I ran to the door behind him, told him in a no-doubt incomprehensible way why I was there, and came close to pleading with him to let me inside, just for a minute. He could, I promised, watch me leave. He hesitated, as anyone in his right mind would have done, but I guess that I looked more pathetic than threatening, and he let me in.

For a moment I thought I was in the wrong building. The stairway was on the other side of where I remembered it being, and the hallway ran straight to the door of the man in the white robes, rather than to David's, which was next to it and behind the stairway. But I looked at David's door and had a flash of clear memory of coming in, late at night. The hallway had always been so bleak, but I knew that I'd find a kind of peace and safety behind the door, where David would be sitting quietly, watching T.V., waiting for me, no matter how late it was.

Guys

I wrote something in my blog about trying to get back to my old life: *...returning for the first time after David's death to one of the bars I used to spend a lot of time in before I met him, sitting alone on a barstool under the blue lights in the early evening as the band was setting up, feeling, for the first time, anger instead of grief, or as a different manifestation of grief. Old friends tried to talk to me, but I could barely speak; they had become intrusions, and I hated them for it. I hated the lights, I hated the music, and I hated anyone or anything who wasn't David, or a means of bringing him back, and I went home early.*

At the time I wrote that, I hadn't yet rediscovered the returned letter that I'd written to David's half-brother Steve. The letter, written two months after David's death, reminded me of two specific incidents from that time that make very clear my feelings about getting involved with anyone else. The first also reminded me that at some point early on in my relationship with David I'd made a conscious decision that I wanted to be with him—that I'd started to think of time spent with other men as a waste of my time:

I got a call just now from a guy I sort of used to go out with before I met David. He was OK but I always had a feeling that he had something missing in his personality. Like sensitivity. A short time after I met David I woke up with what's-his-name one morning and before I even opened my eyes I saw David's face in my mind. And that was that. Just like me to fall in love with someone who's dying...Anyway, I'm going out to meet this guy for a drink out of sheer boredom. I'll probably get disgusted and come home early. Actually, it's a certainty.

The second incident, about which I'd also forgotten, made me laugh:

...It's 1:30 in the afternoon and I'm just getting around to having breakfast at a loud Mexican restaurant near my house. A friend from work is coming by later to play pool and mess up my house. I guess I befriended him because he reminded me in a very superficial way of David (he's about the same age, basically). He's an ex-drug addict, but now he's working as a substance abuse counselor and trying to construct a more "normal" life—job, car, apartment, etc. In two weeks he's decided I'm his best friend...As I said, he originally reminded me in a vague way of David, but he's not David and lately I have very little patience for most people who aren't David...A funny thing happened, though. A few days ago he was at my house and decided to stay over because it was late and he lives far away. We'd gone out for dinner, and when we came back a plant in the room where I keep David's picture and things just fell over (this happened at David's funeral, too—my friends had brought a big pot of flowering branches and left it next to the casket; it had stood there all day but suddenly when we were all standing around talking it fell over too...). Frank (my friend) asked how the plant had fallen over and I just pointed at David's picture. It was a joke (I think), but it scared the hell out of Frank and clarified any misconception he might have had that I was going to sleep with him.

After David was gone I was no longer interested in the tawdry serial relationships I used to find myself in during the bar-hopping days before I met him, and barely interested in ever getting involved with anyone again, regardless of David's suggestion that I get married and have children at some point. It seemed likely that the part of my "burning amphitheater" dream in which I was getting married, although I didn't even know who I was marrying and was going through with it only because it was time and because it would somehow make things easier on everyone, would be the most likely way in which things would actually eventually play out.

But about six months after David's death I rather passively allowed myself to become involved with an Egyptian man who drove the van for the next AIDS agency I had started to work for, and who, during the three years I lived with him, became increasingly addicted to a substance similar to crack (dealing with a heroin addict—especially one on a methadone program—is a piece of cake compared to dealing with someone who does crack, and had I known what he was doing when I first knew him I hope that I would have had the sense to stay away). I was still a train wreck, still barely able to speak to anyone, but he let me talk to him about David without judging what had happened between us, or telling me that I had to move on with my life. When we visited the house on Long Island where David's ashes were buried, he would stand at the burial site and talk to David like an old friend, as if he were still close by and didn't need to go anywhere. I could not have been around anyone who tried to make me let go. He was a good person, and fun to be with before the drugs started to change him, but I couldn't help with his addiction, and the relationship ended very badly.

The next relationship was with my husband; we were married in June of 1994.

Handfuls of Him

I'd been thinking for a long time that I started to forget David almost right away, once the initial period of sadness and loneliness had more-or-less passed, and as I allowed myself to get involved with other people. There was the period, in the first few years after his death, when I made some attempts at fulfilling my promise to write a book about him, but beyond that, I believed, I didn't think about him very much, especially after I got married. But while I was working on the blog I found a box of journals that I'd written after my time with David. When I picked one up, it fell open to a page, dated 17 April 1995, on which I'd written:

Easter: five years gone.
In front of Bellevue
Little fists of flame
Gather on silver branches,
Closed, cold.
I couldn't tell you where I've been.

Just before that, I'd written out a list of lines, culled from the stream-of-consciousness exercises that I did a lot back then, at random; most were clearly about David—I'd been, it seems, at least subconsciously thinking a great deal about the day I'd poured his ashes out into the soil on Long Island:

--In this fear I grab another handful of you

--Holding the divine message that nothing can return

--I've spent this year in different towns and tried to tie up
what had slipped in that desperate year when nothing held

--There it was in dust and grains and bit of bone amazing

--The bulk of you sliding down between my fingers

--You are waiting for the rains to take you out of there, the
wind to lift you into sea and separate you from me

--Spoiling the religion I have made around you

This was five years after David died, and less than a
year after my marriage, but clearly the images of my
time with him and just after were still very much with
me.

There was also this entry, written a few days later:

Drowsy and soothed and more or less clearheaded after
waking from a nap with my husband in the last sun of the day
on the first really warm day of spring I think of writing another
poem about you I've been dreaming not today not specifically
about you lately strange things...like finding an old boyfriend
lying in bed with his new girlfriend in a dark messy room and
noticing they are both deathly thin they both have AIDS... the
last of sun is gone but still it's light outside and the summer is
just beginning and none of this is really about you but I wanted
you to know what I've been doing in the past five years and this
is not all of it by any means I've been around so many things
have happened and still in Hampton Bays there's a sinking in
the ground a little to the left of where it should have been the
grass greener there I think I've let it go afraid to dig around you
afraid that if I plant another tree like the first one it won't last
but I'll plant this year again I promise you I'll find a stick and
feed it until the smoke of autumn fires comes drifting up the
beach I'll watch to keep the fever from coming again...It's felt

like a sin to leave you there, the site unmarked, but you have
been remembered.

And finally, on another page on which I was preparing, apparently, to write the poem about watching him sleep in the hospital, there's this, in which I'm clearly thinking about washing his feet in a basin in his room, near the end:

I'm nothing here your feet so heavy in my hands
I wore the gloves I let the love dismember me

What's strange is that after those few entries, written in April and May, there's nothing else until August, when, under the heading of "1995 Part II: The Zoloft Months", I wrote:

I don't know what happened all those months ago. I froze,
and I couldn't stop crying, and suddenly the mere thought of
writing terrified me again.

I don't remember any of that. What I wonder, of course, is if writing about David then started to push me into something like what I started to go through again, fully and finally, in 2006, and if I shut it down, still not quite ready to really let the sorrow of it start to drown me again, still not ready to fully grieve. I was, after all, a newlywed.

New York

At some point after he was released from the federal prison, David went up to Minnesota to meet his biological father. My impression is that he didn't receive much of a reception; I know that it must have hurt him a great deal to have tried to make contact with the last remaining person who might make some attempt at being a parent to him (even though he was already an adult, and no doubt had been made more of an adult than he was ready to be by the experiences of having been in the army, become a parent himself along with a woman with whom it turned out he couldn't live, and incarcerated in protective custody in a federal prison, with an ax-murderer no doubt passing the time in his own cell plotting his death), and who could give him a connection to some kind of cultural identity, and then to find himself, again, not particularly welcome.

But David returned to Minnesota at some point, and in the late 1970's met and married a beautiful (Deedee showed me a picture of her) Chippewa girl after going through hell to get his first wife to agree to a divorce. The girl was just a teenager, half David's age, but their younger daughter tells me that such things were not unusual in the Indian community there at the time.

David's oldest daughter, Christine, explained her understanding of her father's second marriage to me years later:

I think my mother and father were a fling for each other...my father actually called my grandfather and pleaded with him to ask my mother to get a divorce so he could marry his second wife. I don't know if he'd talked to my mom and asked: I suspect he did (based on her "he'd call me up from time to time to check in" comment). She was capricious -- she might have blown him off. But for him to man up and call my grandfather to intercede took enormous commitment on his part. It was like facing a dragon wearing only a loincloth and a coating of gasoline. I think he must have really loved (his second wife), though the relationship eventually succumbed to the plague of drug use. These kinds of moments should count for something too.

Deedee told me that David, his new wife, and their two daughters had stopped by to visit her in Kansas in 1981. They were on their way to New York. Deedee described David's wife as "very sweet...very subdued, and friendly, but shy," and said that their younger daughter, Maggie, who was probably about a year old at the time, couldn't get enough of David; she wanted to be held only by him. That was the last time Deedee ever saw David.

David lived in New York with his wife and daughters, making his living, I gather, through a combination of doing carpentry and plumbing and selling drugs. One thing I did eventually remember David telling me (I think that it was while we were waiting to be shown his apartment for the first time, just passing the time on the sidewalks of the Lower East Side) was that at one point they had all lived in an apartment in Tudor City, a beautiful old complex across from the United Nations. I will never know for sure if it was true (if the money was coming in as he said it was for a while, it was possible), or if it was one of the things he simply wished had been true. Maggie, his youngest daughter, told me that one of the few memories she has of the time is taking a ride with her parents on what must have been the Staten Island Ferry. (That image makes me happy; when I was a child growing up in New York I used to love it when my mother took me on the ferry for an evening ride after she got home from work. Usually, we'd go

206

to Chinatown and have dinner afterwards; maybe David and his family did the same sometimes, when things were still going well.)

Regardless of what David and his wife's intentions may have been, or what their lives were like when they first moved to New York, things eventually went bad. At one point the family moved into an abandoned building. One day, according to Maggie's older sister Angie, David went out to get some food for them. When he didn't return for a long time, his wife went out to look for him, leaving the girls in the building. Someone found the girls; they were put into foster care until they were sent back to live with their extended family in Minnesota. Eventually, after going into rehab (something I don't believe David ever did) their mother returned to Minnesota as well, and moved in with someone else there. Not surprisingly, she had AIDS too, and she died of it as well. (One thing that both of their daughters related is that David didn't tell his wife that he'd tested HIV-positive, and that she only found out when they were arrested together at some point. Of course, it's likely that she, too, was infected by then.)

I know that David tried to see them in Minnesota at least once; both of them remember being told to hide when he showed up so that he wouldn't try to bring them back to New York. David didn't see them, but his younger daughter remembers that she could see his back from where she hid as he tried to persuade her grandparents to let him. That was the last she knew of him.

Angie told me recently that, in spite of everything that happened, she remembers David and her mother as being "good parents" who tried their best to take care of the girls, were loving and never abusive, and made sure that the girls always had plenty to eat. It surprised me that she remembered things that way, as I'm sure that she'd grown up hearing a lot of very negative things (some of them no doubt justified) about David from her mother's family.

Except for the two girls, who may or may not accurately remember how everything happened all those years ago, there's no one left who can know exactly how things went so wrong. I believe that David really loved his second wife and all of his children. The problem with trying to imagine the circumstances that bring about other people's tragedies is that you can never see them as much more than one-dimensional, black-and-white scenes arranged according to a simple, pre-written script, lacking the complexity and depth, the little personal details and interactions, that make them unique to the people who experienced them. Just as no one knew what really happened between David and me on Suffolk Street, no one knows exactly how it came about that he lost the family he made, except to imagine it in the easiest, most simplistic terms—that he and the younger girls' mothers were drug addicts, with very little ability to fulfill anyone's needs except their own. But there had to be more to it than that.

Even understanding that, it's hard for me to reconcile my image of who David was when I knew him with the one of him as a father who had lost his own children, except that, again, being an active heroin addict doesn't lend itself to being a parent. And, as his sister Deedee made clear, he'd also never had a role model from whom he could learn how to raise children as they should be raised. In his own, and his sisters', and even his father's, experience, children were given up, reclaimed, separated from siblings, moved, and left to their own devices with abusive strangers, all based upon the whims of their parents. In David's case, I don't believe that whims, or a lack of caring, had anything to do with it. He just lost control of things, and regretted it until the day he died.

Now I'm almost certain that asking me to write a book about him was David's last attempt to connect with his family and to let them know that, whatever they remembered about him, or had been told by others, there was more to him than perhaps even he himself had been aware until the last few months of his life.

Visits, and the Preacher's Daughter

I also learned from Christine, David's daughter from his first marriage, that David had seen her at least twice after leaving her mother, and that both times, as with so many things in his life, his good intentions and attempts to make positive impressions led nevertheless to disaster.

In an email, Christine had mentioned something about David's wearing a dress shirt and blazer the last time she saw him. There was no occasion for which I could imagine David ever dressing like that, so I asked Christine to explain. She wrote back:

Yes, dark and it matched the slacks. He looked very uncomfortable in the whole get-up. To this day I can see it clearly, in fact, if I don't miss my guess, it was a size too big. And it was a warm day. I was wearing a sleeveless dress.

There was some weird shit going on that day in my house, because they had him sitting in this chair in my grandparents' bedroom, and at first I was not allowed to see him and I got the impression that he had been told what he could and could not do and say, and that he had shown up unannounced.

I was about 7, I think. Maybe 8 but no older.

I was very shy, he was very friendly, it was a big mystery and there was a ton of tension. He was not really a welcome person with my grandparents, and that much was abundantly evident and still is to this day. Just two holidays back, he was fair game at the family dinner table. It was really all strange. I kind of learned to tune it out. I think there were hard feelings for all involved surrounding my mom and such. What I'd call a 'no-win' deal for anyone with a hand in the mix. For the record, my mother didn't do family gatherings either. She also often felt like an outsider in her own family. I guess we can all tell stories about that kind of thing.

The little interaction I had with him, as I recall, was very pleasant. He was always smiling, and friendly in a way that drew folks to him. As a kid you can tell a friendly adult. When I was about 6, I had flown, supposedly alone, to Kansas...on a lay-over he and his girlfriend met me on the plane and flew the rest of the way with me. Sad to say, he was promptly arrested when we got off the plane because of the girl I think. But his mother had something to do with it also because here's what I remember:

We get off the plane and are coming down the hallway. He's holding one of my hands, his girlfriend the other. Grandma is beyond the ropes, leaning against a wall looking mad. We clear the ropes, but before he can say anything, two tall cops step in and separate us, and cuff him. Then I'm with Grandma W. and that's the last I recall. I'd been going out to spend a week in Kansas with her.

When I related the story to Deedee shortly after that, she remembered it, and filled me in on the events that had led to David's arrest at the airport.

Some time earlier, David had driven from Kansas to New York for some reason; given the timing and the fact that Christine was on the plane with him, it seems likely that he'd intended to drive Christine back to Kansas to visit her grandmother himself. Before he got out of Kansas he'd picked up a hitchhiker, a girl who had told him, if course, that she was eighteen. David must have decided to take her word for it, and she rode along with him to New York. Once they got there, David had called the girl's father—who was, as David's usual luck would have it, a minister. The man asked David to bring the girl home, but didn't mention that he intended to have David arrested for statutory rape when they arrived. (David and the girl must have been on the same flight as Christine all the way from New York without her being aware of it until the layover.)

211

Fortunately, David's detective friend (the one who had asked for David's help in convicting the murderer in Kansas) was aware of what happened, and apparently believed that David hadn't—at least intentionally—done anything wrong. (Whether or not he slept with the girl is anyone's guess, but if he was as much of a gentleman with her as he was with me it's quite possible that he didn't. Of course, it's just as possible that he did.) In order to appease the minister, the detective had David put in jail, but released him on a "technicality" when things calmed down.

Still, both stories made me sad. Maybe it's my imagination, or maybe it's the fact that two people who spend eight months living together and giving each other love while waiting for the life of one of them to end can't help but know each other's minds and hearts with an intimacy not easily gained under normal circumstances, but I swear that I can feel David's discomfort, his disappointment, and his embarrassment both times. I can feel his frustration at being, as usual, misunderstood even when his intentions were good. It's painful; even now I have an instinct to protect him, to shield him from being hurt. I know that he wanted a chance to make a good impression on his daughter, and I know that it hurt him to believe that he'd failed. No one could possibly make me believe otherwise; I knew him.

Letter to His Mother

When I met her in New Mexico, Deedee returned to me a letter I'd written a few weeks after David's death to his biological mother, Frances.

It had sometimes occurred to me as I wrote the blog that perhaps the memories that I did still have of David had been clouded by a romanticism to which I fully admit to being prone, that I was creating a David who had never quite existed out of my foggy memories and scattered bits of writing. It wouldn't be an unnatural tendency.

The letter, however, gave me proof that the David I wrote about seventeen years later was the David I'd really known, and that the relationship we'd had was as close and sweet as I'd remembered, and that I really did love him. Until I read the letter, months after I'd finished recounting the story in the blog, I'd remembered nothing of what I'd written to Frances, but the things I told her then were the same things that I would have told her all those years later, and the same things that I'd said in the blog:

Dear Frances,

I'm sorry it took me so long to send this letter and picture to you, but I went away for a little while and I also wasn't sure what to say to you. I'm still not, really, but I'll just see what happens as I go along.

There were a few pictures that I could have sent you, but I like this one the best. It was taken in August or early September, I think, when I had just met David and he was still pretty healthy. People tell me that he looks too sad in it, but I don't really see it that way. I think it just looks like David at his best—kind, intelligent, wanting to be liked and understood. I mentioned that at the funeral—something about how it was his desire for people to like him that was the biggest

213

part of his personality. It used to really upset him when people, even strangers, didn't respond to his efforts to be polite and friendly, or when he was trying to explain something about himself and someone didn't seem to want to listen or care. It was especially difficult for him in the hospital, I think. His illness, toward the end, began to make it difficult for him to speak or think clearly. Sometimes it made him hallucinate frightening things. Although some of the nurses and doctors were kind and understanding, many didn't have the time or patience to try to listen when he tried to express his pain or his fears or what he thought would help him get better or feel more comfortable. That may have been a big part of why he was always so reluctant to go to his clinic appointments or to the hospital when he really needed to. It was hard for me, too, because sometimes I had to guess what he wanted and make decisions for him. Fortunately we had become very close when he was still able to say more, and we'd developed a relationship that often made us both able to know what the other was thinking and feeling. I'm not sure that I did everything as he would have wanted it, and at times I was afraid that I was deliberately going against his wishes when I was just frightened and frustrated, even angry. One thing remains in my mind: the day before he died his homecare worker and I put him in a taxi with his wheelchair to take him to the methadone clinic. The trip was incredibly hard, because David couldn't walk or stand or talk, and he hadn't eaten or been outside for weeks. But it was a beautiful spring day, and in the taxi I put my arm around David and he put his head on my shoulder. There were cherry trees blooming everywhere, and I could tell that David was happy to see them and to be outside after so long. I think that he would have wanted to ride around and look at things for the rest of the day, but we were all exhausted and we went back home. I was still thinking that he might be angry with me, but there was no way to know what he thought. But after a few minutes, while he was sitting in the wheelchair in the apartment, he put his hand out and I took it and knelt down

214

next to him. He squeezed my hand and looked down at me and I knew he was thanking me and telling me that everything was all right between us. I suppose he knew that there wasn't much time left, and I'll always be grateful that in all his pain and weakness he was kind enough to understand that I needed that from him...

It occurs to me that David may have been very different during the time that I knew him than he was when you last saw him. He told me a lot about you and the family and his life before and after he came to New York. I guess I knew that some of what he told me wasn't true, and I've spent a lot of time trying to figure out why he would have lied or tried to hide things from me. In everything else he was always very honest and open, and I trusted him completely and knew that he would never do anything to hurt me or, if he could help it, anyone else. Maybe it had to do with his having been an addict for so long—that lifestyle seems to make dishonesty a necessity and it had probably become a habit that he couldn't completely break. It's possible that he even believed the things he said. I've decided that the story he told me about his life was the one he wished was true. He knew that he was dying and he didn't want to think (or have anyone else think) that his life had been a failure or a waste. The stories he told me (I'm not saying it was all untrue—the facts were sometimes just distorted or rearranged) were all very sweet, and some were very painful, too (especially the ones about his adoptive parents). Maybe it says something about his character that the things that he wanted to be true about his life were all good. I never wanted to tell him that I didn't believe some of what he said. That's why I never got to tell him that it didn't matter to me what he had or hadn't done, because what I knew of him from being with him almost every day for eight months was enough to make me love him. Some bad things happened in my own life during that time, and if it hadn't been for David's kindness and concern and wisdom things would have seemed much worse. I knew that he'd do anything for me, and I would have done the same for him. It

215

seems almost impossible that I could ever have a relationship like that with anyone else, and I'll always miss it.

Anyway, sometimes I am tempted to find out who David really was before I met him, and to ask you about it. I'm not so naïve that I think that he was always a saint, and I'm sure that he used to raise hell on a regular basis. He did say that there was a lot he was ashamed of, but he told me once that when he was first in the hospital for AIDS he made a decision to "get rid of the bad parts of his personality" (which he apparently managed to do)...

He was always talking about children (he even suggested once that I get myself pregnant one way or another and that we move to the country somewhere and raise the child—it was pretty much fantasy at that point because he was so sick, but it was a sweet idea and I wish that there'd been time and a way for us to do it). (That reminds me to tell you that, although David and I used to sleep together almost every night, he never really tried to make it sexual. It was very nice, and it would have obviously been dangerous for it to have been otherwise, but I do admit that sometimes I regret that it had to be that way.)

Anyway, whatever happened in the past between David and you and his family, he would have wanted you to know that he got to the point where he wished more than anything that things had been different...Maybe someday I'll ask you to tell me some things about him, but right now it seems that it wouldn't do any good and that it would be a kind of betrayal.

David's picture is in front of me as I write this. You might find that his eyes seem to follow you around the room wherever you go. I haven't had much experience with death, and I don't know what to believe about what happens after someone dies. It's still hard for me to understand that this is permanent— sometimes I come home and expect to find a message from David on my answering machine. I wish that I could know for sure that he's not too far away and that he's watching me and knowing how much I miss him. I wish that I could see and

216

talk to him, and I'm always very happy when I dream about him.

By next weekend I hope to have found a flowering tree and buried David's ashes beneath it near the beach. I hope that you think that's appropriate, and that he'd like it. After that I'll feel that everything is finished except for missing him and trying to fit this whole experience into my life somehow. It seems that nothing will ever be the same again, and that everything I do or see or feel will somehow refer back to knowing and loving David. I hope I don't seem obsessed or ridiculously sentimental, although maybe I am right now.

It's late and I guess there's not much more to say, except maybe thank you for bringing David into the world and I hope that you're able to see beyond the waste and horror of his death and know that in spite of some of the things he may have done in the past he was a good, kind man and in his own way he did what he could to make the world a little better...

A Life

I've heard, many times, the argument that there are plenty of people who, in spite of suffering abuse and neglect as children, grow up to be successful adults, people who make the "right choices." It's true. David, early on, made bad choices (although it seems to me that he may have chosen drugs over insanity)—choices that couldn't be taken back, that came to obscure all the other possibilities that might have been available to him, that denied him, to some extent, the "luxury of feelings"—that eventually ended his life.

As far as I can tell, David had very little experience with love throughout most of his life, or at least when he was a child; if that hadn't been the case, he may well have made different choices. The thing that's remarkable to me is that, when love was finally offered to him, undiluted and unconditional, and at a point at which he was no longer so consumed with the need to get high that he couldn't recognize it, in the last months of his life, he knew what to do with it.

Everyone makes bad choices; some get caught in one way or another, and others don't. I made some of the same choices that David did, without even having had the excuse of abuse, instability, and a lack of love in my life. But David got caught, and I, for whatever reason, didn't.

What I had in those eight months was David, wrecked and burned clean, like driftwood, doing what he could to "get rid of the bad things in his personality," trying to live, finally, a life resembling something normal and good. The man into whose dark, calm eyes I stared in the hours before his death, speechlessly seeking forgiveness and perhaps getting it; whose essential sweetness I must have sensed the day I met him; whose kiss I declined, because I knew that a kiss would not be enough, and I was afraid; whose breath I'm trying to hold, was and is David distilled almost down to who he was at the moment of his birth and the moment of his death, nearly free of the ugliness, the cruelty, the stupid tragedies, the mistakes, the lies, and his own weaknesses—the things that had brought him all the way down to who he was the day he walked into my office and sat down at my desk and began to talk.

What I'm trying to do, I think, is to simply give him back in his life in a way that he'd be able to recognize as something that mattered. Because, like any other life, it did.

Gifts

Every so often, just when I thought that there could be no possible remedy to a pain that had by the winter of 2006 become at times physical as well as emotional, no resolution to the grief, and no respite from the feeling of trying, over and over, to reach through a barrier I couldn't see, something would save me. It might be a dream, or suddenly being able to find someone connected to David, alive and happy to talk to me, or a song, or the chance recovery of a sweet memory. At first, the relief, although welcome, was temporary and isolated, but gradually things began to happen at shorter intervals or even connect with each other by unexpected and what seemed like magical threads so that their accumulated weight began almost imperceptibly to tip the scales in the direction of hope, and even joy.

The first of these miracles came at 4:30 one morning in the early winter of 2006 when, having once again been unable to sleep, thinking about all of the terrible things that David's sister had told me so far about what he'd been through as a child, wondering again if I'd come even close to mitigating any of it in his last eight months, and still miserable with the guilt of the ways in which I'd let David down, I checked my email with tears running down my face again, and received the blessing, the affirmation that what I remembered and felt was real, that I'd been waiting to hear for sixteen years. It came from Deedee, to whom I'd sent what I'd written about David so far:

I have read all that you have sent me; it's both tragic and beautiful. I have often been extremely grateful through the years that you were there for David when he needed someone to love

220

and to love him...It's a good thing you managed to find us, there is a reason that this happened, and that it happened now, I hope that you know that I feel that way. I don't think that you ought to even remotely consider that you 'failed' David in any way—quite the opposite—you were his salvation. And, in spite of the fact that he passed during your temporary absence from his room, I'm confident that he knew he was not alone.

And then, a few days after Christmas, at my mother's house in Florida, I had another dream about David. I wrote it down as soon as I woke up:

I came to a little black-and-white town, and I had the sense that it was a town from David's past, or maybe Brainerd back in the days when his grandparents lived there. I came around a corner, trying to figure out which era I was in, and saw cars from the 1960's and 1970's—a VW Bug, Camaros, Mustangs.

Next I was in a booth in a restaurant. There was a plate glass window behind me, and I was sitting with a big group of people. We were waiting for David, and everyone knew how excited I was, and how desperately I wanted him to show up, and they teased me about it a little. I glanced behind me and saw him getting out of a taxi outside, smiling, looking as I've been imagining he looked around the time that he testified against the murderer. When he came in, however, he was the David I'd known—thin again, obviously sick, but still handsome. He sat down next to me in the booth and I put my head on his shoulder and put my arms around him and we just hugged each other for a long time. His body felt so real, and so solid, and warm; I couldn't stop touching him.

Later we were in various places nearby; he was saying hello to old friends, but the important thing was that we were together. At one point I went downstairs to a bathroom, as I used to at our Spanish restaurant on the Lower East Side, to brush my hair. I remembered that I didn't have a brush, but it was alright because my hair was short, as it had been when David was alive; it had never been all that necessary to brush it.

When I came back upstairs, David and I worked on some kind of religious wax statue, using a mould. Apparently we were supposed to get it done before we went anywhere else, but it kept falling apart, and we were laughing about it. Finally we finished, or just gave up, and then we were back in the booth, just holding each other. Without really meaning to, and so quietly that I didn't think he'd hear me, I whispered, "You're mine." He did hear me, though, and he answered, "I'm yours." It was the first time he'd ever spoken to me in a dream.

I woke up then, but without the usual sense of having been interrupted. I opened my eyes and saw that the sky was getting light, in delicate pinks, oranges, and blues, and for the first time in a long time I was happy that another day was beginning, certain that David was talking to me, and telling me what I needed to hear—just as he'd done when he was alive.

And finally, a year or two later, David's daughter Christine wrote to tell me about a dream she'd had; she felt that it had been a message to me from David:

I was on a pier at a beach, but it was like a California beach, not like the ones in NYC, because the pier had a short spit of sand, and then there were rocks and the ocean, and I had the impression the shelf dropped quickly and the water was very deep. It was just before sunset. I was waiting for someone. It was hot, humid, and there was a trade wind breeze. Don't ask how I knew it was trade winds, just in the dream it seemed it was.

So time passes, and this shadow falls over me. I turn and realize it's my father, looking like he did the last time I saw him, in a white dress shirt, dark slacks, and a dark blazer. He points to the water and says, "Look." At first I don't see anything. He says, "Look closer. See what's in there so you can tell her."

Okay, I'm always game for crazy stuff. I stare harder. At first the water is black. I sort of relax into looking at it, and then it clears, like a ray of light is shining down into it. I see this car, nose first in it: a late 70's model - I think a Mustang. I think to myself, I need to see this better. The water rolls across it in waves. I focus, the beach fades away, and then I'm in the water seeing the car level with where it is as opposed to looking down.

There is a skeleton in the driver's seat, and I know it is my father. The seat belt was keeping it in the car, but the waves have loosened it. The skeleton is in danger of falling apart.

Then, I realize there is a woman holding onto the driver's side door latch on the outside of the car. She is angled down; her feet are up towards the water line and the light. The light is shining brighter now. I realize she is attached to the car, but the car needs to come out of the water.

Then, I am somehow above this, still in the water, and I am seeing the car and woman getting pulled out of the water into the air but the force that is doing it is invisible.

I get the impression the woman is you. The skeleton my father. The car has held you both prisoner beneath the waves, and the current was about to wash you both out to sea, but something about the new light being shined on something that has been hidden allows it to come out into the open at last. There is a TREMENDOUS amount of force that is released when the car and the people clear the water and hit the air, like Jupiter releasing a breath.

Then I'm standing back on the pier leaning on the railing watching the car, et. al., *resting on the rocks and sand of the small shore. My father nods to me as if I'm supposed to now do something with this knowledge, and vanishes.*

And I can only think... that coming out of the water into the air is bringing the story, your story, out into the air without having to hide it anymore. It was like if you don't reflect, you're in danger of forgetting. And the act of coming out gives you an incredible amount of power as a result.

Maybe that—a dream offered like a gift from David's daughter almost twenty years after his death,

223

and one in which I'm holding my breath in order to get to him before he's lost forever, and before I drown myself—was a clue to what David had meant when he'd said that he needed someone to hold his breath for him, and the final answer to my prayer:

I asked for a day, or an hour, or a few minutes, or—failing everything else—a dream. An opportunity, a little time to have one more chance to do what I needed to do and say what I needed to say to make things right with David.

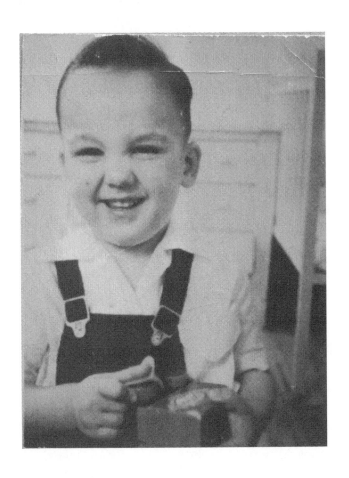

PLAYLIST

These are some of the songs that I listened to during my eight months with David, and songs that, since then, always remind me of him in one way or another. For me, they've always been as much a part of the story as anything else. For readers who like to listen to music while they read, this would make a good soundtrack:

Feelies, "On the Roof"

Lloyd Cole and the Commotions, "Charlotte Street"

Lobo, "I'd Love You to Want Me"

T. Rex, "Mambo Sun"

Bob Mould, "Sinners and Their Repentences"

U2, "With or Without You"

The Animals, "We Gotta Get Out of This Place"

The Association, "Never My Love"

Patti Smith Group, "Dancing Barefoot"

Grateful Dead, "Friend of the Devil"

The National, "Bloodbuzz Ohio"

Bob Dylan, "Shelter From the Storm"

Bob Dylan, "Simple Twist of Fate"

Staind, "It's Been Awhile"

Badfinger, "Day After Day"

Bruce Springsteen, "Streets of Philadelphia"

Johnny Cash, "Hurt"

Bruce Springsteen, "For You"

Todd Rundgren, "Dust in the Wind"

Crazy Horse, "I Don't Want to Talk About It"

Cowboy Junkies, "Come Calling" (His Song)

Cowboy Junkies, "To Love is to Bury"

Sinead O'Connor, "Nothing Compares 2 U"

Rolling Stones, "Wild Horses"

Chris Isaak, "Wicked Game"

k.d. lang, "Constant Craving"

Ringo Starr, "Photograph"

The Band, "It Makes No Difference"

Gordon Lightfoot, "If You Could Read My Mind"

The Animals, "Don't Let Me Be Misunderstood"

Grateful Dead, "Unbroken Chain"

Jefferson Airplane, "Coming Back to Me"

Bread, "Everything I Own"

Joan Baez, "Diamonds and Rust"

Cowboy Junkies, "Angel Mine"

Mazzy Star, "Fade Into You"

Pearl Jam, "Alive"

U2, "One"

Amos Lee, "Windows Are Rolled Down"

David Bowie, "Heroes"

America, "I Need You"

Glen Campbell, "Wichita Lineman"

For additional information, links to the above songs, photographs, etc., please visit the blog:

http://holdingbreathmemoir.wordpress.com/

ABOUT THE AUTHOR

Nancy Bevilaqua was born in New York City. After studying English Literature and Creative Writing at Reed College and New York University, she worked for ten years as a caseworker and counselor for people with AIDS, the homeless, and people in drug treatment programs.

She married Lorenzo Bevilaqua, a photographer, in 1994, and in 1998 their son, Alessandro, was born. A few years later Nancy became a freelance writer, specializing in travel; her articles, essays, and photography have appeared in *National Geographic Traveler, Coastal Living,* the South Florida *Sun-Sentinel,* several in-flight magazines, and many other publications.

Nancy and Alessandro now live in Florida, where, although she loves the beach on which she lives, Nancy still dreams nearly every night about New York.